Reboot Hiring

Reboot Hiring

The Key To Managers and Leaders
Saving Time, Money and Hassle
When Recruiting

Katrina Collier

WILEY

Registered Offices
John Wiley & Sons, Inc., 111 River Street, Hoboken, NJ 07030, USA
John Wiley & Sons Ltd, The Atrium, Southern Gate, Chichester, West Sussex, PO19 8SQ, UK

For details of our global editorial offices, customer services, and more information about Wiley products visit us at www.wiley.com.

Wiley also publishes its books in a variety of electronic formats and by print-on-demand. Some content that appears in standard print versions of this book may not be available in other formats.

Library of Congress Cataloging-in-Publication Data

Names: Collier, Katrina, author.
Title: Reboot hiring : the key to managers and leaders saving time, money and hassle when recruiting / Katrina Collier.
Description: Hoboken, NJ, USA : Wiley, 2024. | Includes index.
Identifiers: LCCN 2024019688 (print) | LCCN 2024019689 (ebook) | ISBN 9781394278138 (hardback) | ISBN 9781394278152 (adobe pdf) | ISBN 9781394278145 (epub)
Subjects: LCSH: Employee selection. | Employees—Recruiting. | Social media.
Classification: LCC HF5549.5.S38 C65 2024 (print) | LCC HF5549.5.S38 (ebook) | DDC 658.3/111—dc23/eng/20240514
LC record available at https://lccn.loc.gov/2024019688
LC ebook record available at https://lccn.loc.gov/2024019689

Cover Design: Wiley
Cover Image: © freshidea/Adobe Stock
Author Photo: Courtesy of Rosie Parsons

Set in size of 13/16pt and Janson Text LT Std by Straive, Chennai, India
SKY10081342_080624

For Sophie Power, my huge-hearted neurospicy friend, writing advocate, and TA attestant.

Contents

Foreword

Hiring in 2024 is heading towards a critical juncture: recruiters are overwhelmed by thousands of resumes they receive for jobs, while jobseekers complain that they have to send hundreds and hundreds of applications into a void and that most often they never hear back after submitting an application. Hiring has become a lose-lose endeavour.

I recently wrote the book, *The Algorithm: How AI Can Hijack Your Career and Steal Your Future*, showcasing how broken the hiring system is, especially in the age of AI. In the book I document the rise of AI and algorithmic hiring tools quantifying and ranking jobseekers. I uncovered actual evidence of wrongdoing in many first-generation AI hiring tools. My book revealed that not only are many AI tools broken and some have gender and racial bias, but often recruiting is as well. Hiring managers and recruiters often don't know what the most important skills and capabilities are that they should look out for and many new hires quit after joining a new company.

That's why I applaud Katrina Collier, who has taken her experience helping recruiters and talent acquisition professionals, and has written a book for the managers and leaders in the business. Her book is almost like a sequel. I discovered what is going wrong and she is taking these hard-earned lessons and is translating them into advice, so managers and leaders can do a better job, find better hires, and make the process not suck, for themselves, their recruiters, and for jobseekers.

She lays out how we can fix the process with the humans in the middle: starting with recruiters and hiring managers working together to fix the dreaded job description, with clear goals and deadlines.

I love Katrina for giving actionable and meaningful insights, even going so far as sharing specific tools one can use and detailing which processes might work, down to the best questions managers and leaders can ask to understand what exactly they need in a new recruit. She also advises letting talent acquisition professionals sit in on job interviews, so that they gain a deeper understanding of the role. She even recommends what kind of assessments companies should use and which to avoid and has a nifty checklist of all the tools and questions to ask, at the end of the book.

Her recommendations will undoubtedly help recruiters, hiring managers, and jobseekers to all have a better experience! A more human, thoughtful experience, which is needed in the hiring field, which is bound for a major reckoning, since more and more jobseekers now use algorithmic tools to automatically apply – leading to even more application overload on the recruiter side.

I hope Katrina's advice will be helpful to all managers and leaders so they partner better with talent acquisition and that this trickles down to the jobseekers, a start to a much-needed reboot.

Hilke Schellmann
Emmy award winning investigative journalist,
Author of *The Algorithm*, and Assistant Professor
of Journalism at New York University

Introduction

Technology Won't Fix Your Hiring. But You Can

Managers and leaders want an easy fix. They want to believe that technology will provide an effortless way to reduce the cost and hassle of talent acquisition. They think they can automate it because they assume it takes little more than an interview to recruit successfully. Some are so blissfully unaware of what it truly takes to hire great people that they also believe prospective employees will willingly hand their career to an emotionless bot.

People are peculiar, fabulously so, and recruiting them isn't straightforward. In *Reboot Hiring*, I offer an alternative based on my 21 years of experience: a free solution within your control. I will show you that implementing technology without fixing human-created problems already hinders hiring. I will agitate your reality and show you that fixing these human issues is the only way to save time, money, and hassle when recruiting.

The choice is yours.

In preparation for writing this, I searched for books on the human collaboration and communication issues that impede hiring, but I couldn't find any. In some ways, this makes sense; talent acquisition is a relatively new function that is evolving rapidly. Many managers and leaders are unaware of this pace of change, the enormous opportunity, or their value. Instead, they treat them as a costly service, an inconvenience best avoided, unaware that this self-sabotaging behaviour makes recruiting clunky, expensive, and wasteful.

Technology also won't fix managers' and leaders' inability (or even unwillingness) to articulate who they need to hire. Poorly written job descriptions become vague job advertisements, barely standing out in the noise generated by 5 billion internet users. They attract few and unsuitable applicants. Time is wasted reviewing and assessing irrelevant people while the manager or leader silently hopes they will "know it when they see it". Bias creeps in, frustration rises, and time and costs escalate. *And it is all avoidable.*

Alas, you won't be able to fix people's struggles when writing their resumes; they are simply challenging to compose. If attempting to automate the matching of these poorly written documents against the job specification with AI, I share research that reveals why, for now, this is better left to humans. Plus, relying on technology is pointless if you are not confident in knowing who you need to hire and how to effectively keep people in the process while your competition also woos them.

To solve this, through this book, I plan to convince you of the value of partnering closely with your talent acquisition professional and spending more and wiser time at the start of the process so the whole thing becomes less tedious and wasteful. Importantly, by improving the partnership and process, your and your company's reputation won't hamper future hiring.

In the following pages, I will show you that a shift in perception and smarter use of your time will deliver an efficient, cost-effective, and stress-free hiring process for everyone.

Recruiting in 2024

In 1991, I secured my first full-time job at the National Australia Bank in Sydney through a newspaper advertisement. I began in a suburban branch run by a deeply unpleasant manager who reduced me to tears within days over a minor infraction and had the second-in-charge so stressed that she vomited each lunchtime. Of course, nobody cared about employee morale and engagement or its impact on productivity in the 1990s.

We stayed because we were afraid of not finding another job. We endured it because this was before the internet significantly impacted employment. We remained because we could not see the countless other available jobs without today's Google and online job boards. One also never left a job without another lined up – a job for life was still a thing. Thankfully, I was transferred and discovered that not all managers and leaders behaved this way.

In 2003, I relocated to London, UK, and found my way into the recruitment profession via, ironically, another newspaper advertisement. Over the last 21 years, I have experienced the enormous change in talent acquisition created first and foremost by the internet and, latterly, technology. The power dynamic shifted as people began using online job boards and joining social networks to find work and discover employers. Recruitment agents lost their secret books of contacts as companies started using LinkedIn to find and hire without them. Sourcing evolved as the curious learned to find people on niche sites and forums. Mobile and social recruiting became the buzz, just like AI is now.

The internet irreversibly opened the door to your company; it's too late to shut it. Employees and job seekers now have a voice and know that working for you and your company is a choice. It is naïve to think that applicants won't be looking at your social footprint, either. The power is theirs: it will never again be a company's, as bitter a pill as that truth is for some leaders to swallow.

Today, people don't have to tolerate poor management or leadership when they can browse on their phones for a new job. As they search, they can hear from employees directly; there are no more polished C-suite statements to deceive them; they can find the truth. Company reputations matter; CEO ratings impact applications. Standing out in the posts of billions of internet users is challenging for companies. Until they mess up, that is. Today a viral TikTok video can quickly destroy an employer's brand, making current and future hiring hard and losing them applicants and clients.

In these pages, I share many examples of the transparency created by the internet so you can learn from them and avoid similar costly mistakes. You will see Glassdoor reviews and posts from Blind, and though my love-hate relationship with Reddit's Recruiting Hell is intense, I chose its posts because they illustrate problems I hear about repeatedly from job seekers. Besides a few outliers, it is a supportive community of 631,000 members sharing their job-seeking experiences. You may wish to disregard negative posts or reviews as petty, but I chose examples that clearly show the power of employees' and job seekers' voices and their reluctance to endure mistreatment in 2024. I wish I'd had such a community 33 years ago.

What Awaits

Perhaps it is because I am Australian, and over two decades in the UK haven't softened that. Maybe it is because

I champion the underdog: the poor candidate stuck in the hiring process. Perhaps it is because I respect your irreplaceable time and that you chose to purchase this book. But I don't hold back from asking tough questions or making bold, reasoned statements in these pages. I believe, on some level, all managers and leaders know that people are their differentiator and that they could do this hiring malarkey better.

Due to the internet and, often, the use of the wrong technology, talent acquisition has become overly complex and arduous. It doesn't need to take such an emotional toll on the people running its gauntlet – people who end up down or depressed, or worse. It doesn't need to cause burnout for the talent acquisition professionals caught in the middle. And it doesn't need to be a chore you avoid or loathe, as many in talent acquisition tell me you do!

The companies I witness consistently hiring and – critically – retaining great people treat their recruiters as close hiring partners, spend more time at the beginning confidently articulating who they need, run interview processes that are sensible and respectful, interview fewer and more suitable people, and don't hate it. This could be you, too.

Most of my work is with companies, managers, and talent acquisition, so this book leans that way. If you don't have a talent acquisition function and work with agents, substitute "agency recruiter" when you read "talent acquisition partner" because partnering with them effectively and thoroughly articulating the need is still crucial. If HR or procurement prevent you from directly communicating with their vetted list of agents – without valid business reasons – resolve this for the sake of current and future hiring.

In these pages, you will also discover why current technology does not have the capacity to replace recruiters and why it will never solve the actual reason hiring fails: communication and collaboration. If that's your plan, stop and read this first; it could save you from making an unwise investment that costs you both candidates and customers.

You are busy, but skip ahead at your peril. I have been succinct without losing key elements, and this book only works if you understand the moving parts. It may be tempting to bypass chapters where the title doesn't resonate or you think you have a grasp of the topic, but humour me and read the many gems I have tucked away in the stories and examples. Except for the last chapter, which you could read at any point, the rest are best read in order, so I can leave you with the formula to save time, money, and hassle when hiring.

Ready to reboot your hiring?

1

Recruitment Alignment Meeting

"Oh no! What is this meeting in my calendar? I don't have time for this! It's all on the job description. What do they want? Go away!"

Have you ever thought this when someone from Talent Acquisition tries to schedule time with you? If so, you are far from alone if the idea of attending this meeting fills you with dread because you already have enough on your plate. Nor will you be the first manager or leader to find recruiting people for your team challenging, even scary, and wish it was less hassle.

I penned this book for managers and leaders who dislike, perhaps even hate, hiring as a way to give it a reboot. I plan to convince you that this meeting makes or breaks the entire hiring process. Getting it right, or even 50% better, will make the whole thing less loathsome and tedious. Heck, you might even enjoy this meeting when you learn why it matters, what to take, why it's the key, how to confidently articulate who you need, and how much time, money, and hassle you can save by creating a solid hiring partnership.

But Should You Be Hiring?

I know! This is an unexpected change of thought. Here you are with the sign-off to hire a new team member, and I am asking you to pause. Even now, it is worth pondering this question for a moment.

The 2020s have been a rollercoaster for employees! Countless companies over-downsized in an unprecedented pandemic, and too many overhired in 2021 into 2022, which led to layoff upon layoff from mid-2022 to now, early 2024. That's before considering the companies that implemented technology and transformation, which created even more layoffs. With this in mind, expect an exceptional recruiter to challenge you on the hiring need, because should you be hiring externally at all?

Damaging Layoffs

A compassionate talent acquisition professional won't want to mess with people's lives. People aren't numbers on a spreadsheet; they are not a commodity. They are human beings with thoughts, feelings, and emotions. Layoffs are linked to a greater risk of suicide and mortality in the decades after being cut, and employees without existing health conditions are 83% likely to develop one in the 15 to 18 months after redundancy – stress-related illnesses like hypertension, heart disease, and arthritis.[1] This is before considering the drop in employee morale and the damage to the mental health of the remaining employees who fear they, too, will be cut.

In a transparent search-engine-led world, you must also consider the harm redundancies have on your employer and consumer brands. Take the January 2024 round of layoffs at Wayfair, which included the termination of Andrena Mcmayo, who received awareness of the situation while on her way to chemotherapy.[2] To the company: a number on a spreadsheet and a confession of overhiring from the CEO. To everyone who saw the posts online, i.e. future Wayfair customers: a woman with stage 4 metastatic breast cancer fighting for her life who now has to somehow pay for her medical insurance while jobless.

Unsurprisingly, just 36% of employees say they approve of Wayfair's CEO on Glassdoor, a drop of 40% since 2021, possibly due to his December 2023 inference to the press that he has lazy employees or the poor hiring decisions that led to yet another round of layoffs.[3, 4] The publicity gets worse, too, with videos like 'Wayfair's Shameful Layoff – Can You Lose Your Job on Disability Leave?' appearing on YouTube.[5] At the time of writing, it had received over 52k views and hundreds of comments from former customers and employees in just eight days. I will no longer shop at Wayfair, and am not the only one with this sentiment. Tiempos DePaz added in the comments, 'Wayfair has gone downhill, and I used to purchase a lot from them often. This is the nail in the coffin.'

The cycle of overhiring and mindless layoffs must stop. The cost is too high.

In late 2022, I spoke with ServiceNow's Senior Director of Talent Acquisition, Alia Khattab; she shared that she had intentionally not hired two team members, even though she had the sign-off. Reflecting on this, she told me,

Lots of my decisions come from instinct, but with this one, I used data from our game-changing Talent Intelligence function and the projections we had with Finance. At ServiceNow, robust operational and financial rigour around hiring allows us to plan resources effectively. The data showed that in 2023, we would be hiring at half the headcount growth we had during the post-COVID bubble; balancing my team productivity and headcount growth for FY23, it was clear that we would be above capacity. Therefore, I consciously decided to cancel my two additional hires, which was the best decision for our team.

Toby Culshaw, author of *Talent Intelligence: Use Business and People Data to Drive Organizational Performance*, advises companies:

Conduct thorough labour market research before expanding your workforce; overhiring without foresight risks jobs. Assessing labour market trends, availability of required skills, and projected hiring needs will inform a smarter talent acquisition strategy. Rushing into overhiring can leave a company overstaffed when business contracts and necessitate painful layoffs. Doing your labour market homework before ramping up helps prevent the high costs of hiring, training and then cutting employees. Talent Intelligence allows building a workforce that scales judiciously with actual demand.[6]

Internal Hires

Recruiting internally first is wise; it is more cost-effective, and the individual's performance and productivity are proven. Also, a 2011 study by Professor Matthew Bidwell found that new external recruits have significantly lower performance evaluations for the first two years, are paid 18–20% more, and have higher exit rates than promoted employees. Though they also bring more experience and education, hence the higher salary, and are promoted faster.[7]

Retention   Ignoring the visibility issues across large companies, which internal mobility software can assist with, the attitudes of managers and leaders often hinder internal transfers. Some feel that they own their team members; they are bogged down in the weeds instead of looking at the benefit to the company of retaining a star employee. This behaviour creates resentment and a restless employee who will soon be perusing the internet for their next role, while their lack of motivation impacts those around them. In fact, a 2023 study from Culture Amp found that 52% of people leave organisations for development opportunities, so don't stand in the way of a team member's internal transfer if it means they'll stay.[8]

Before you contemplate recruiting externally, consider internal options. Who has transferable skills? Who is smart enough to pick up something new? Would the company benefit from backfilling a role and retaining this particular employee? These are the questions to consider.

On hiring internally, Alia Khattab added, 'Internal employees with the potential to succeed should be fast-tracked through the hiring process. If your internal employee is 70% there, appropriate learning and coaching will soon bridge the 30% gap. That's a win-win for talent retention and growth.'

Side Note: Benchmarking Employee Experience and Human-Centred Designer Steve Usher warns against benchmarking externally when the plan is to fill the role internally.

> *Though a manager or leader may seek validation on their thinking regarding an internal candidate, want to compare skills gaps and cost differences, or make the business case, using company resources to interview, for the sole purpose of benchmarking, is not free. It is also unkind to inflict the emotional rollercoaster of an interview process on an individual who will never be hired, someone who could become a client or speak poorly of the experience in niche networks.*

Alternatively, many companies offer benchmarking services that won't risk your or the company's reputation, and there are also free online tools to obtain salary information.

Renaming "the" Meeting

Now that you have considered these points and you are definitely hiring externally, it's time to discover the recruitment alignment meeting and its impact on your time, money, and workload.

When I polled talent acquisition and recruiters on LinkedIn about the name they use for the make-or-break meeting that starts the hiring process, I heard too many options. Unlike how they use one word, candidates, to cover prospects, applicants, interviewees, etc., the opposite is true for this meeting. It has too many ill-fitting names, which detract from its importance.

So, in particular, I am banishing:

- Job brief – because this meeting cannot be brief! By the end of this book, you will know why this meeting is where you invest your time to save bucketloads of it later.
- Kick-off – because your responsibilities don't end there; getting a new employee over the line takes a strong partnership.
- Intake strategy session – even though I call it that in my book, *The Robot-Proof Recruiter*, far too often, it was cropped to intake.
- Intake – because you're not ordering a pizza.

US Talent Acquisition Manager Jennifer Stockton shared, 'We stopped calling it an intake meeting because it felt like it was communicating an order process. Whereas the meeting is to align on job requirements, market realities and partnership commitments.' Exactly! So to ensure that this meeting sets the tone for a successful hiring partnership that saves you time, money, and hassle, I call it the recruitment alignment meeting through this book.

It's Not on the Job Description

If you want to waste your irreplaceable time and company resources—while ruining your and the company's reputation – interviewing countless people who aren't quite right, then avoid the recruitment alignment meeting by saying that it is all on the job description. Or, you could just ignore the numerous meeting requests until they become so fed up with the disrespect that they close the requirement, and you have to start over. And don't think they won't; any self-respecting talent acquisition professional won't allow a colleague to ghost them.

However, if you want to save time, money, and hassle, you will never fob off your hiring partner. As you will read through this book, talent acquisition or external recruiters know the realities of the hiring market, and they have questions for you that don't belong in the job description. Plus, this meeting is for far more than just agreeing on who you need to hire.

So, though you may have used the current specification to secure sign-off for the position, they need more to persuade prospects to become applicants; they need the minutia. I have dedicated a whole chapter to 'articulating the need' (Chapter 4) because I want you to be able to confidently describe who you need – not want – in the recruitment alignment meeting. Then, you can create an accurate and realistic job description together, which can be used confidently throughout the entire hiring process.

Banish People-Pleasing

If you want the recruitment load lifted off your plate, create an environment where your talent acquisition professional can challenge and guide you! Don't force them to say yes because they are intimidated; some newer professionals might be nervous speaking to a senior manager or executive. Park your job title and seniority to one side and become equals; you are the expert in your domain, and they are the expert in recruitment. Let them query your assumptions, ask questions you think are inane or tedious, show you another way, and educate you on the possibilities.

In Chapter 3, I share different qualities to look for in your recruiter, whether they are in Talent Acquisition or external. For now, know that if you want the hiring process to be easy and smooth for all parties, you don't want or need a yes-person working on your role. A people-pleasing recruiter or talent acquisition professional will not lighten your workload. If they are frightened of you – it happens! – then they will go along with everything you say even though they know recruitment will fail. You want someone who makes you think, who is confident, curious, and unexpected.

Plus, if you don't let them challenge you, you can negatively impact their mental health, which is unwise when they are the person responsible for helping you hire your people. I have a podcast that supports my memoir with interviews with people who have healed and improved their mental health. A talent acquisition professional asked if they could talk about their crippling imposter syndrome. They said, 'Over the last 18 months, I have spoken openly to more colleagues, past and present, who have said they have felt the same. Unsurprisingly, many are working in recruitment and being asked to find unicorns or perfect people who do not exist!'

Reading her application to speak on my podcast made me incredibly angry. Partly because this person believes imposter syndrome is something to cope with, which it is not. But mostly because they wouldn't be looking for a unicorn – the industry term for a non-existent candidate – if the manager treated talent acquisition as a partner, respected their knowledge and experience, and listened to marketplace reality. Instead, they are expected to waste their time and the company's money, damaging their mental health, all while the manager blames the talent acquisition professional for a shortage of applicants.

German-based Talent Acquisition Leader Amanda Lamont believes:

> *that senior business leaders' tendency to view talent acquisition as a service, instead of a partnership, undermines their ability to challenge unrealistic hiring expectations. This is especially true for junior recruiters, who are still gaining confidence in their influencing skills needed to persuade hiring managers to make more realistic candidate profiles. Talent mapping is the key to bridging the gap; managers and leaders can better support recruiters by believing the data.*

Finally, if you wonder if yours are too "nice" after reading this, train them! Send them on courses and to conferences, show them my newsletter, buy them my other book, and invest in coaches and mentors. Make your life easier by developing the people you rely on to find, attract, and convert your new recruits.

Bogus Must-Haves

By the end of this book, I want to have convinced you to ditch writing lists of must-haves that send talent acquisition professionals off on unicorn hunts that ultimately lead to them doubting their own abilities.

As I share in Chapter 7, LinkedIn may not necessarily be the place to find the candidates you need, but it can provide an idea of what is possible. If your talent acquisition partner has access to LinkedIn Recruiter, encourage them to run a search during the meeting to gauge how likely it is to find a purple squirrel – another term for a non-existent candidate – and if it is wise to remove the "must haves" they can learn on the job.

However, many simply rely on their experience and industry knowledge to challenge your expectations into something realistic. Swedish Talent Acquisition Manager Sofia Broberger shared:

Because I am confident and have extensive knowledge of my industry, if the list of must-have requirements is absurd, I can tell the managers; the trust is established. I ask them to pick three and then ask questions like, 'So if they have A and C but not B, will you see them?', etc. It helps them solidify their thinking.

Similarly, Bulgarian Recruiter and Founder of Remote IT World Yanislava Hristova said, 'When asked for too many must-haves, I rely on my experience and convince managers using examples of previous and similar roles. I navigate them to what is possible by asking many questions about each requirement. I want to know why it is there to reduce them to something feasible and realistic.'

It is simply par for the course to be questioned and challenged in the recruitment alignment meeting; ignoring your talent acquisition professional's expertise and data is self-sabotage. Yet, I hear horror stories of unnecessary escalations by unreasonable managers and leaders, especially in countries with complex hierarchies. Ultimately, they want to help you fill this role. If they know what you are asking for will yield few results and waste your time, why wouldn't you listen to them?

But if you genuinely believe that someone with twelve-plus must-haves exists, guide your talent acquisition partner to the data. Show them the evidence and the places where they can find one. Surprise them with facts that set them up to successfully find, woo, and convert this unicorn into an applicant.

Preparation Is Vital

You have other priorities, I know! Hiring is probably your least favourite task, especially when you're down a team member. Your team may have flight risks from those carrying the load while the vacancy remains. There is pressure to deliver projects to keep clients and other business units happy and secure your bonus, of course! Filling this role is another time-consuming task you don't need when your manager is on your back about deadlines, and the mundane paperwork that goes with being a boss is piling up.

However, the more you prepare, with the knowledge you gain reading this book, the more you can give the recruitment alignment meeting your quality, focused, and efficient time. With the reward that you free up countless hours that would be wasted interviewing people you would never hire, hours that can be better spent on more enjoyable tasks.

In Chapter 4, you will learn how you can better articulate who you need, and if it is possible to invest time before the meeting to ponder the people specification, that would be helpful. If it has been some time since you submitted the business case for the new hire or if it is a backfill from an employee's departure, this would be especially helpful. But, if you haven't had time to do that, that is okay; just tell them. Take the checklist I have created for you with you, and together, go through all the questions until you are satisfied you have developed a specification for the person you *need* to fill this role effectively.

Work It Backwards

In 2023, I delivered a two-day design-thinking workshop for a brand-new vet practice that wanted to establish everything crucial for recruiting staff, particularly the people it needed to open its doors and start trading.

The first thing I asked was, 'When are you opening?' as I rolled out a calendar – sometimes it helps to see it printed – and I placed a sticky note on opening day. Then I asked those who would be involved in hiring, which worryingly relied heavily on just one person, if they had any holidays booked. I blocked those dates off with more sticky notes. Working back from the opening date, we started considering likely notice periods for new employees, the time required for onboarding, the expected interview rounds, etc. It was startling seeing an opening date that seemed like many months away become, in reality, inadequate time to recruit 25 people unless we created a unique hiring experience, which is what happened over the balance of the workshop.

Start with the end in mind. When is the absolute latest date that the person can start? What is the average notice period for this role? Count back those weeks or months. What is your company's onboarding period? It's likely a week, so take that off, too. How much time do you have left? From this, your talent acquisition partner can help you determine when you need resumes, the deadline to provide feedback, when screenings will occur, when manager interviews must happen, and so on. Be savvy: block out the time there and then, in the meeting, ready for those interviews.

On the site formerly known as Twitter, Donna, a social media agency owner, shared:

> *Had an interviewer [the company owner] eat a bowl of cereal, slurping and chewing loudly, during a Zoom once. Like, dude, if I did that, you'd stop the interview. He then asked me to summarise my resume because he "didn't have time" to look at it in the week since he'd set up the Zoom – red flags. I didn't send him my portfolio afterwards. No, thank you.*[9]

To ensure you don't have an interviewee withdraw, please block out an extra 10 to 15 minutes before the interview to read the resume. It is also a great time to take a few deep breaths to centre and calm. You may also want to tack ten minutes on at the end of the interview to jot down your thoughts while they are fresh in your mind.

If this sounds like a lot of time, remember that you will always interview far fewer people when you give a detailed recruitment alignment meeting. That's our aim!

Get Your Ducks in a Row

While I was bemoaning how long some companies take to create a purchase order, US recruiter, Debi Easterday stunned me into silence. She shared that she had a contractor who was offered a role in August but could not start until January due to delays with procurement:

> *The manager had budget allocated and approved, but processing the Statement of Work could only begin when a contractor was identified and offered. It took an incredible 12 rounds of signatures to gain approval, and nobody within the procurement department understood the urgency or the impact on the candidate experience. It was tough keeping the contractor from taking a different job, too!*

Imagine starting this process from scratch if the contractor had withdrawn, which most would have. Delays like this are costly, especially when project delivery relies on hiring in skills swiftly. Often, ridiculous processes are legacies from previous leadership, and though they are no longer fit for purpose, they remain unchanged. If your company has a similar procurement obstacle course that seems unwarranted, address it because it will be impacting the brand and the bottom line.

Thankfully, this company realised its bottleneck, and Debi added that the process has improved significantly, 'It now takes less than a month, though, with the right automation and notifications, I am sure this could be shorter still.'

In this instance, Debi's company was already an authorised supplier because using an agency that was not approved could also create delays. So, before you involve a recruitment agency, it's crucial to check with Talent Acquisition or Procurement if the company has been vetted and approved. Doing so will avoid delays and ensure the company doesn't agree to excessive fees and unreasonable payment terms.

If you want to know why Talent Acquisition has reduced outside agency use or will no longer let you use your favourite supplier, speak to them. Open communication is critical to keeping the company's reputation intact and candidates in the hiring process.

What's the Cost?

For several years, I have encouraged talent acquisition and recruiters to ask managers and leaders, 'What's the cost?' The answer helps them prioritise roles, as they seldom work on just one, and it gives them something to coax you with. OK, nag, but it is for your own good.

Now, I want you to consider the financial and human implications momentarily.

My favourite question, which many feel is too direct, is: 'What is the cost to the bottom line every day that this role is open?' This figure won't always be easy to calculate, but if you had a project on the line, it might be easy to calculate that it is £5000 per day, for example. Then, when your recruiter promises to get resumes to you on Monday, and you agree to respond by Wednesday, but it is Friday, and you haven't, you know the delay has cost the company £10,000.

What costs can you estimate if you can't calculate a daily figure? Is there a deliverable dependent upon it in another part of the company? How does missing the deadline impact that business unit? What about client delivery? What is the value of the current work, and have you been discussing future projects? Keep thinking until you find the cost.

What about the cost to you? Does this hire help you secure a bonus or commission? Do you have a promotion on the line? How do you personally benefit from hiring this new team member? What about work-life balance? Will this recruit mean you can reduce your hours and have more time outside of work?

Finally, there is the human cost to the team. What's the cost to the team every day this role is open? Are others picking up the slack? Do they need to work extra hours? How is that impacting morale? Do any of them have feelers out for a new job? What would happen if you lose a few key members of the team?

Of course, you might go through all of this and find that the cost is so low that you wonder why you are hiring, but I hope that if the reason for recruiting has been appropriately considered, this won't be the case.

Now it is calculated, take the cost, write it on a sticky note, and keep it in front of you. Look at it when someone from Talent Acquisition chases you. It will remind you of its importance when it feels like another chore in the middle of a hectic day.

Interview Balance

During the recruitment alignment meeting, you will agree on the preferred interview loop with your talent acquisition partner; in Chapter 6, I will fully detail the considerations you must make regarding interviews. As always, be open to being challenged; they only ask for your benefit and the sake of the candidate experience.

Interview Loop

The interview loop is the sequence of conversations and tests used to assess someone's fit for the role. It varies from open hiring, where companies like Greyston Bakery hire without interviews, to processes with so many steps that great people withdraw if the role doesn't match their values or mission. For example, my friend Steven is two months into a hiring process with one company and has met 17 people so far. The only reason he tolerates the indecision is that it is a sector he would like to work in, and once in, he has every intention of changing it to a streamlined and inclusive process.

This Glassdoor interview review for Biotronik Australia did make me chuckle because many wouldn't call three interviews in two weeks tiresome. However, the offer-declining reviewer makes an interesting point, 'Long and lengthy—too many interviews and too many questions for a simple role. First interview was with HR, then the team lead and a manager, and then with manager, HR and dept manager. It was tedious and not necessary for a customer service role.'[10] Three interviews do seem a lot for an entry-level role, and it is curious that HR attended twice. But this review also evokes all of my Gen X-ness as I sense bias rising; this new generation has different expectations. As leaders and managers, we have to consider adapting or, like Biotronik, we could be starting the hiring process over.

Steven's and this reviewer's situation could leave the impression that the company has a toxic blame culture.

The *Oxford Review* defines a blame culture as 'an environment where people, or groups/teams, are frequently singled out and blamed, criticised, and fault is apportioned for mistakes and errors. This tends to result in people being reluctant to accept responsibility for their actions and mistakes because they are afraid of criticism and reprimands from their managers and leaders.'[11] In such an environment, having many interviews means you can blame someone else if the new recruit fails and avoid being singled out and humiliated.

In contrast, managers don't fear short interview loops in a company with leaders who provide abundant emotional support and use emotional intelligence and compassion. Plus, once you are clear and confident about who you need to hire, which I intend to give you in this book, you won't need many interviews to decide.

Two-Way and Generous

British recruiter Jo Scott shared a LinkedIn post addressing some agency recruiter behaviour, but its sentiment also relates to managers and leaders hoping to keep people in the interview loop.[12] So, paraphrasing:

> *Candidates are grown-ups with rent to pay, mouths to feed, and opinions to which they're entitled! Your candidate will not do something because you want them to; they'll do it if they think it's right for them. Interview no-shows happen because they don't have a relationship with you, they do have one and struggle to let you down, or they just don't think you are important. Respect that this is their career, 8 hours a day, five days a week.*

In Chapter 2, I will discuss how the internet flipped the power from the company's thinking, 'Be grateful you have a job", to the employees' and candidates' thinking, 'Be grateful you have employees.' Where once you could grill an interviewee relentlessly and they would still accept your offer, times have changed. Poor interviewer behaviour is no longer tolerated and can end up online, hindering future recruitment. Interviewees expect you to sell the opportunity and the company to them, as you might to a potential client, and give them plenty of time to answer your questions and ask their own.

Later, I will provide many questions and ideas to help you create and articulate your person specification, but interviewees are human and, therefore, quirky. They may want to know more. What else would they like to learn to help them decide about the job? Exactly, it could be anything. Unless you give them time to ask, you won't know. And what you say here could be the thing that makes them accept your offer later or politely withdraw, which saves you the expense of a failed hire and beginning again.

If your interview loop includes your C-suite, they should uphold your hard work and the courtesy of a two-way interview, even if they are less invested in your hiring process. Otherwise, you could receive a review like this one for Secureframe from a senior management interviewee who had completed three interviews and an assignment before meeting the CEO:

Every interview was informative and professional except for the CEO. He was late to the interview, provided no context about himself or the company, no small talk, and didn't even try to get to know me. We didn't even discuss the assignment, which I thought was part of this interview. He left no time for questions, which was so disappointing! An interview is a 2-way conversation; the company is trying to find out more about you, and you're trying to gauge if this company is what you want in your next role. Word of advice: offer training to your managers AND CEO on how to interview.[13]

Imagine how frustrated the manager and talent acquisition felt having to find the time to start over.

There are AI tools for online interviews that can help with interview fairness by producing live meeting notes so you can focus on the conversation, ensuring it is two-way and generous. Metaview's AI creates notes for recruitment alignment meetings and interviews, and can benchmark how much time the candidate was given to speak against previous interviews. Humanly's AI co-pilot automatically generates interview notes and, through something akin to a flight recorder, provides insight into the evenness of the conversation and highlights possible bias. Similarly, Bright-Hire's interview insights and AI-powered coaching can help you level up interviews and reduce bias.

Include Talent Acquisition

People & Talent professional Sophie Power shared with me that she has had managers refuse to explain the role adequately because they thought she didn't understand their function, which seems counterintuitive!

Besides sharing information in the recruitment alignment meeting, what about inviting talent acquisition to join some interviews? In my recruitment agency days, I regularly attended interviews with candidates and found them eye-opening. I would learn about client projects and development opportunities not written in the job description or covered in the meeting. Managers and leaders would light up as they shared their joy at working for the company and their future plans.

By walking the floors, meeting the teams, and attending interviews, I gained knowledge I then used when speaking to prospects, which made selling the opportunity easier and conversion to a new hire more likely, saving everyone's time.

The other benefit of talent acquisition attending a few of your in-person interviews is that they can – if you're open to it – provide feedback on your style and areas needing tweaking. If you are new to interviewing, they can provide excellent support and instil confidence to help you overcome any novice nerves you might encounter as you gain experience.

Caveat: this can only occur if the talent acquisition function is appropriately resourced and must only happen if the interviewee is aware in advance that they are attending the interview. They must be comfortable having talent acquisition there because too many – particularly unexplained – bodies in an interview can be intimidating. I also recommend that the recruiter sit beside or at a 90-degree angle from the interviewee for in-office interviews.

Offered, Silver Medallists, and Rejected Candidates

My aim is not to teach you how to interview, assess, offer, or knock back candidates because plenty of training and books are available to help you learn this. However, and though it might seem strange to drop this in here, I want to touch on the subject of offered, nearly-offered, and rejected candidates because how you treat them impacts the employer brand and future hiring.

Offers

If you have done your job during the interview loop, and the applicant has had plenty of opportunity to consider the role and remuneration, you as a boss, the team, the company's mission and values, the potential for growth, etc., the offer process should be smooth. You want to discover what motivates them personally about this job; it's wrong to assume that people change jobs for money alone. Finding this out will significantly increase your chances of converting them into a new recruit.

During the recruitment alignment meeting, get clear on who needs to be involved in the offer process and negotiation, what wriggle room there is on the remuneration, and who will contact the interviewee with the good news.

Rescinded Offers   There are countless posts online saying something like, 'I had an offer rescinded because I asked for documentation on their benefits package instead of immediately saying yes.' I shake my head at the wasted expense of restarting the hiring process just because someone wants all the facts before making a vital life decision, and the company didn't like it. Please do not cancel an offer because people need more information, time to consider it or to speak to their loved ones; few people make snap career decisions. Remember when you last changed jobs; recall the emotions at play and the people involved. Be empathetic and kind; companies spend weeks asking people to jump through rounds of interviews, and the least managers and leaders can do is reciprocate. People needing time or information does not indicate a lack of excitement to join or that they're not grateful!

However, you may have to rescind an offer for extraordinary reasons. I hope it will be the exception, not the norm because we are playing with people's lives. The worst experience I heard of was of a South American man who, after receiving an offer, sold his house to move his entire life to the Nordics, only to have the offer rescinded a few days before he was due to start. Imagine the heartache, the stress, and the massive financial loss.

If this must happen, consider how the news is delivered. To be kind, the manager or leader should tell them on a call, but if an email is sent, please carefully consider its wording.

A Reddit user shared that they received and signed a job offer on Thanksgiving, only to have the start date pushed back twice.[14] Finally, they received the news that the offer was withdrawn via an email from an anonymous person in 'the talent acquisition team'. The email coldly states that 'with the end of the year approaching, the company has decided to put an end to all new positions on that specific team'. Worse, as someone noted in the comments, 'Terrible it happened, but adding to check out their website for other opportunities is just laughable.' A responsible company wouldn't have started the hiring process or could have identified options in other teams for this offered candidate. The post has 3500 upvotes and 360 comments, and all are impacting the employer brand.

Silver Medallists

How you treat the applicants pipped to the job is also important. They could be great for a future role, joining another team, or the one you want to hire if the preferred candidate turns you down. Transparency is better than stringing them along, pretending that they are still in the running if they are not, for now. Most people understand that they are not the only person in the recruitment process, and honesty builds trust.

Feedback

The 2023 #End Ghosting Report found that 87% of ghosted applicants feel down or depressed – 31% moderately and 12% severely.[15] Wanting closure is natural; with the right technology, it is possible to reply to every applicant. As every job is attached to a talent acquisition team member, it is also kinder to sign off the email with a name and avoid using 'no-reply' email addresses; this allows people to connect to the talent acquisition professional on LinkedIn or join the talent pool for future job opportunities.

However, everybody who has an interview deserves more personalised feedback for the time, money, and energy they have invested in the process. During the recruitment alignment meeting, always agree to give feedback to your talent acquisition professional so that you never knowingly leave an applicant down or depressed. It is better for personal and company reputation that the interviewee can discuss the feedback, so encourage them to speak to them rather than just send an email.

Partnering to Success

The final part of the recruitment alignment meeting is agreeing on how you will work together throughout the hiring process. By the end of the meeting, besides all the role particulars, you will agree to something similar to the checklist on page 26. You will know what you need to do, and they will know what they need to do. As I will explain throughout this book, the more engaged and responsive you are, the more time you save down the line.

Talent acquisition	Manager or leader
☐ Source/advertise	☐ Communication preference
☐ Pre-screen	☐ Interviews
☐ Ways of working together	☐ Feedback
☐ Driving the process	☐ Ultimate decision

In-house Talent Specialist Christian Payne shared, 'I explain the end-to-end hiring process in the intake meeting, including agreeing on who posts the role and aids candidate attraction. Posts from managers stand out in busy LinkedIn feeds, so I encourage them to be active. Lately, we have had great success when managers share job videos or carousels.' In Chapter 7, you will read more about easy post ideas that help with talent attraction.

Recruitment isn't transactional. People aren't commodities. You can't withdraw a new human from a vending machine. They are complex. Resumes don't fall from the sky. It takes work to find, attract, woo, keep in the hiring process, and successfully convert a prospect to a new employee who actually turns up and starts on day one.

In Chapters 2 and 3, I will demystify Talent Acquisition, which is a strategic function when established correctly and empowered. Then, I will explain what to look for when choosing its people: those who play such a significant role in hiring your team – the people who decide the company's fate. As tempting as it could be to jump ahead, it is essential to read to deliver on this book's promise: that you save time, money, and hassle when hiring.

Lastly, treat your talent acquisition partner as an administrator or a service provider, they will invest more time with the hiring managers who treat them respectfully and create ease. It is human nature. They work on many roles; make your life easier, be their favourite.

And remember, your talent acquisition professional doesn't just sell the benefits of working at the company and the role; they sell you, too!

Chapter Summary

- Layoffs damage people's mental health, employee productivity, and the company's reputation and bottom line. Only recruit when you are confident it is the right move.
- Treat your talent acquisition professionals as administrators and service providers, and you will waste time and money and create unnecessary hassle for yourself.
- The best recruiters and talent acquisition professionals form strong partnerships with their managers and leaders and challenge you so you hire who you need, not want.
- Interviews need to be balanced and realistic because candidates can choose from many other opportunities visible online. All applicants merit closure; interviewees deserve feedback so they are not left down or depressed.
- Your talent acquisition professionals sell you too; be their favourite and reap the benefits.

2

Decoding Talent Acquisition

Due to the transparency created by the internet, both you, as the hiring manager or leader, and your Talent Acquisition function can make or break your company's ability to hire successfully. Both now and in the future.

On the positive side, the internet shifted the hiring dynamic from one where companies relied solely on advertising or agencies to one where they could find people online and invite them to apply. But it also irreversibly moved the power to employees and candidates. People can now choose where, when, and how they want to work. Finding other jobs online and reading employee and candidate reviews are easy. Simply put, people don't have to work for you!

If you are considering skipping these few chapters, humour me and read on because whether your company already has a Talent Acquisition function or not, it is worth (re)discovering its impact on the company. And why, in a world with over 5.3 billion internet users, creating a partnership with recruiters is the only way to reboot your hiring.[1]

Talent What?

Generally, managers and leaders understand what most of their business functions do. Departments that have existed for decades, like Finance, Sales, Marketing, Customer Service, IT, Production, Operations, etc., are familiar. Most also have some understanding of what Human Resources (HR) does; after all, the department has been around since the 1950s.

In contrast, Talent Acquisition is in its infancy, and where it sits and operates best is up for debate. In my experience, HR professionals can be baffling, and I'd be rich if I had a dollar for every time I heard how much they dislike, even hate, hiring. This disdain is concerning if your

HR department is responsible for hiring or managing the Talent Acquisition function.

Digging into this, I found that recruitment is low on, if not omitted from, the agenda of many of the official HR bodies and conferences, which makes a definition like this one from Workable worrying: 'An HR department is tasked with maximising employee productivity and protecting the company from any issues that may arise within the work-force. HR responsibilities include compensation and benefits, recruitment, firing, and keeping up to date with any laws that may affect the company and its employees.'[2]

When HR is too focused on protecting the company and policing, it works against hiring and retention because the transparency created by the internet makes it easy for people to leave or make a different choice. Today, people seek leaders and cultures that align with their values, and the more confident people are at sharing the realities of working for a company online, the harder it is for those companies who forget that they are run by people, not spreadsheets and shareholders, to retain and recruit.

In the distant past, it was okay to have HR responsible for hiring because they only managed third-party recruit-ment agencies or sifted through job applications, but this changed with the arrival of the internet. Talent Acquisition has emerged as its own entity with distinctive skills, pro-viding companies with a unique opportunity to attract and hire the best people for roles directly. In my opinion, Talent Acquisition and HR are akin to siblings. If I were advis-ing your company I would, controversially, establish Talent Acquisition outside of HR: where it can function as a close partner but also plug directly into other functions like Sales, Marketing, Communications, and Finance. Hiring the right people is so crucial to your company's success that Talent Acquisition deserves a seat at the table – right next to HR.

However, Talent Acquisition has a perception problem that worsens when busy managers don't find the time to speak to or understand who they are and why they matter or refuse to partner with them on hiring. When the people you recruit can impact your ability to deliver work or projects, risk your ability to receive a promotion or bonus and, of course, decide the fate of your company, this behaviour is self-sabotaging. In a people-driven hiring market (candidate-driven), your job isn't the only one available, and it is hard to see it among the noise and distraction online. It takes proactivity to find, source, attract, engage, and convert someone from an 'identified prospect' into someone who is 'actively interviewing' because those 5.3 billion internet users create a lot of rivalry for attention.

Your company's competitive advantage is its people, happy ones more so. According to new research from economists at the University of Warwick, happy people are 12% more productive.[3] Plus, research from Wrike, who partnered with Atomik Research to survey workers across the United Kingdom, France, Germany, and the United States, found that the majority of the happiest employees in the US, the UK, and Germany all rank 'doing meaningful work' as the number one factor for their happiness, and that four out of ten employees have taken a pay cut at some point in their career, to accept a job that made them happier.[4]

There is little more meaningful work for those in Talent Acquisition than offering employment and watching someone start and grow within a company. It certainly makes up for rejecting people from the hiring process, which is a massive part of the job and emotionally taxing. Imagine the enormous impact on your company's hiring if the people in your Talent Acquisition function were happier. You could create this by partnering with Talent Acquisition, even 50% better than you are now. And most importantly, save yourself a bucketload of time, money, and hassle. This book will give you a formula that will allow you to reboot hiring by investing a little more time at the beginning to create a successful partnership and a lot of ease down the line.

But let's get real for a moment: there are a lot of false beliefs when it comes to hiring. For managers and leaders, this happens because, on most days, you are doing your job, which doesn't involve trying to get the attention of countless prospects or speaking to hundreds of potential new employees. Other than the many approaches you receive via LinkedIn each month, it is unlikely you have as good a picture of the current hiring market as your recruiters do. So, let me dispel some myths.

Common Misconceptions

When I crowdsourced the common misconceptions between managers and Talent Acquisition, my LinkedIn post and inbox were overloaded. Many recruiters thought I could write a trilogy, but I will spare you and keep this brief.

As you have already chosen to read this book and, more importantly, this chapter, I think you have an open mind, but if any of the following resonates a little too much, know that people who choose to work in Talent Acquisition usually want what is best for the people they hire, the company, and their managers and leaders. Most of these are simple communication and collaboration issues, which mobile devices have proven that technology won't fix, and interestingly, the themes are similar worldwide.

False: Recruiting Is Easy

> *There's an assumption that you just need to map the market, send LinkedIn messages, and people will come flocking.*
> —Katherine Mountford, Professional Services, Australia
>
> *My hiring managers underestimate the challenge and effort that it takes to acquire top talent. They think it's an easy job to communicate with someone and attract them to the company, and they overlook the concerns a candidate has when changing jobs.*
> —Mohammed Alduhan, eCommerce, Saudi Arabia

If only recruiting was easy! Imagine how much time, money, and hassle you could save. The reality is, though, as more people go online each year, it gets more challenging to gain and hold someone's attention. Consider how many messages or emails you received this week. How many remain unanswered? How many were from recruiters this week? Did you answer those? Even though your device was within reach, giving you easy access to your messages and emails, did some stay unattended? Some that matter, like those from family and friends. Because unlike back in the day, when a phone was just a phone and incessantly rang until answered, mobile devices make it easy to ignore notifications and ghost people.

In my book, *The Robot-Proof Recruiter*, I talk extensively about the noise and transparency created by the internet. I encourage recruiters to be vigilant and creative about where, when, and how they contact potential recruits.[5] But even the most hyper-personalised and targeted message can remain unanswered because people have choices. Not replying, engaging, or applying are all valid options. Even during layoffs or downturns, people still have alternatives. They don't have to work for you or your company.

Floor Nobels, who works in recruitment in The Netherlands, replied to my post and added, 'It's wrong to think you can hire very experienced professionals with very junior recruiters!' She is right. Assuming they have little life experience and training, people find it too hard to trust an entry-level recruiter with their career and live-lihood, and they feel the same about automation and AI.

Wrong: Tech or AI Can Do It for Us

> *There is an assumption that recruitment is a linear process that can be automated with a good piece of AI. This belief overlooks the emotional elements needed, the nurturing, the relationship building and the sheer number of variables within any hiring and decision-making process.*
> —Aylin Abdullah, Tech Sector, UK

Take a moment to reflect on your last career or job change. Remember the emotions at play. Think about the time you invested in jumping through the hurdles of the hiring pro-cess and making your decision. Recall who you involved in your decision-making process and how your new job could impact your partner, children, pets, or other loved ones. Remember any fears you allayed about changing jobs, start-ing, and possibly failing, or simply making a poor career choice. Rarely is changing jobs an emotionless process.

In the early 1990s, I worked at the National Australia Bank when they started installing automatic teller machines, and the engineer cheerfully told me that cashpoints would soon replace me; they didn't. In fact, there are still tellers in the bank three decades later because some customers like interacting with a human, even for something as mundane as a cash transaction. There are also still cashiers in the supermarket for commonplace grocery purchases.

Most people will be unwilling to trust their careers fully to AI or automation. Countless job seekers post complaints about AI in applicant tracking systems; they feel it is doing them a disservice already. In 2019, I touched on the bias apparent in HR tech in my first book, and Hilke Schellmann delivers a startling read in her 2024 book, *The Algorithm: How AI Can Hijack Your Career and Steal Your Future*.[6] Believing that people would prefer to deal with technology for something as crucial as their livelihoods and that, therefore, you can do away with recruiters is unfounded.

Plus, the most critical and broken part of the process, the one focused on in this book, will never improve with technology alone.

Incorrect: Talent Acquisition Are Order Takers

*It is wrong for managers to believe that we have only to take their 'order' and not question their wish list when discussing their vacancy. I am there to challenge them and help them figure out what they **need** as opposed to **what they want**.*
—Zsuzsa de Koning-Szabó, Civil Engineering, the Netherlands

The perfect candidate doesn't exist. Certainly, not one that can meet an endless list of must-haves and who will immediately fill your top performer's shoes.
—Somyen Mohanty, Tourism, India

Over the years, thousands of recruiters have heard me say, 'If you want to take orders, work at Pizza Hut!' As I shared in Chapter 1, an order is a job description with an endless list of must-have skills. The recruiter's job is to help you articulate who you need, not want, which means questioning you to ensure that recruitment will succeed for all parties.

It may seem that all those must-haves will save you time or that the perfect person is out there willing to join you, your team, and your company, but it is unlikely. If your talent acquisition partner lets you continue your "order", you will waste time, money, and energy interviewing unsuitable people; time, money, and energy you could have spent upskilling the person who was a 70% match for the role and had the right attitude for your company's culture and mission. You could also damage your company's employer brand.

Untrue: TA Only Manages Recruitment Agencies

Talent Acquisition is not just there to manage an agency pipeline of candidates. Let Talent Acquisition decide when to engage agencies and which ones to use. After all, we're not telling tech teams which coding languages to use.

—Clive Smart, Tech Sector, UK

On top of the misconception that managers often think anyone can recruit, they also underestimate the expertise required to be a good Talent Acquisition partner. Talent Acquisition has evolved into a strategic function that can have a far deeper impact than 'just' staffing your team. Once this misconception changes, everything changes.

—Juliette Rouquet, Professional Services, Germany

As mentioned, the HR function did manage agencies in the past, which might continue in small companies or those without the volume to warrant a dedicated talent acquisition professional or function. However, as I will explain in Chapter 3, when companies give Talent Acquisition the resources and tools to function optimally, they can become proactive and strategic. They can create seamless processes, save the company money, build market maps and talent pipelines, protect the employer brand, improve candidate experience, and more.

Mistake: Just Post an Advertisement!

> *It's a mistake to believe we won't find someone if we are not advertising on one of the main job boards. There are many ways to attract people to a company, and advertising or using job posts is just one of them, and not to be solely relied upon. Give us time to explain the other more productive options and why they will make things easier.*
>
> —Adam Cicchetti, Tech Sector, Australia
>
> *It's a misconception that hiring is as simple as writing a job description or, worse, copying one that's been around for a while and posting it on a job board.*
>
> —Steve Levy, Financial Services, USA

Type your job title, location, and the word 'jobs' into an internet search engine and hit enter. How many are there? Thousands? Tens of thousands? People with skills that are in short supply, especially those in STEM, Healthcare, and even Hospitality post-pandemic, are spoiled for choice and rarely scour job boards looking for a new role. Instead, they're being actively sourced by talented talent acquisition and recruiting professionals or referred by friends and former colleagues.

Critiquing an online employment marketplace, Australian talent acquisition leader Stan Rolfe shared this post on LinkedIn in March 2024:

> *In 2023, we hired over 70 people across various video games industry roles. So far in 2024, we've hired 20 more. In 2023, we hired two people from SEEK. So far in 2024, none from SEEK. One grad and one IT Support in 2023 was it. We spent over 15k with SEEK for two hires. Our success was through our amazing sourcing team, referrals, and direct outreach efforts.*[7]

Posting on a job board may seem logical, but it could prove a costly waste of time. Instead, ask your talent acquisition partner, who should possess the data and experience, to advise if it will produce results. When Talent Acquisition is permitted the time and the appropriate technology, they can create and engage with a database of people who have already expressed an interest in working for your company.

In the first half of 2023, I delivered part of a recruiter upskilling programme for a company rolling out a brilliant new human-centred hiring process. It should have been a success, but instead, others, without listening to the expertise of the Talent Acquisition team, decided to implement the wrong applicant tracking system. At the same time as we were training, the company was rolling out a new HR information system (HRIS), and to sweeten the deal, the vendor offered a "free" applicant tracking system (ATS). Like most HRIS ATS add-ons, it is unfit for purpose; it is so poor that instead of asking each applicant role-specific knock-out questions, it only allows the same questions for all roles globally. Due to the industry's attractiveness, this lack of functionality creates a deluge of unsuitable applicants for every role. Recruiters now waste hours wading through to find the best applicants, making delivering a better candidate experience nearly impossible. This costly mistake also shows how free seldom means free.

Nobody knows talent acquisition better than the team that spends 100% of its time recruiting. Trust that they know whether you should advertise and whether the chosen technology is fit for purpose.

Inaccurate: Top Talent Wants to Work for Us

> *It's surreal that managers think they can put in minimal effort and get a top-rated star candidate.*
> —Amie Ernst, Artificial Intelligence Sector, USA
>
> *Some have the belief that working for their organisation is so desirable that it offsets dubious behaviour!*
> —Ed Han, Financial Services, USA

Top talent, or as I prefer to call them: 'people who know their worth', know they have choices and it doesn't have to be your role or company. Even through turbulence, they won't accept unreasonable hiring processes, poor hiring manager behaviour, or unsavoury employment conditions. It's not the noughties: companies no longer have control over where, when, and how 'top talent' will work.

Countless factors make a company desirable or a candidate want to work for you, but as this has been such a hot topic of debate in 2023, let's consider location for a moment.

Despite extensive layoffs worldwide in the tech sector, a recent Deloitte survey revealed that nearly 90% of industry leaders thought recruiting and retaining talent was a moderate or major challenge.[8] Leaders also said two problematic areas were 'finding people with highly sought-after skills and helping younger workers thrive in an evolving workplace'. Some stated that those who entered the workforce remotely during the pandemic are reluctant to work in the office.

Many polls on LinkedIn show how many people reprioritised where they work during the pandemic. One poll, 'How many weekdays are you currently expected to work from an office?' received over 10,000 responses, and fewer than 20% of respondents were required to be in the office full-time; 39% have full flexibility, 23% just 1–2 days per week, and 19% 3–4 days.[9] Another poll by *Business Insider* asked, 'What's the optimum number of days to go into the office per week?' and of the 26,182 who voted, 25% said none, 67% said 2–4 days and just 8% voted for 5 days per week.[10]

The comments cite examples of people resigning when mandated to return to the office full-time or companies giving up their commercial properties because employees won't return to arduous commutes. Many comments show that this all comes down to trust and communication between employees and their leaders. But the main issue is that if your company has or is considering mandating a full-time return to the office, as these polls show, you are massively reducing the available pool of people willing to work for your company.

The best thing you can do for your hiring is to accept the advice of the people who know what candidates, especially those highly sought-after ones, truly want. Remember that the hiring process is two-way; be sure to truthfully sell the opportunity and give candidates plenty of time to consider their next career steps.

Rarely True: Our Brand Attracts New Employees

Managers often place too much importance on corporate branding, believing it will attract talent. It won't.
—Miguel Mayorga, Tech Sector, Germany

The strength of a consumer brand is not the same as your employer brand.
—Derek Murphy-Johnson, Manufacturing, USA

There are many places to find employee and job seeker reviews online, including Glassdoor, Kununu, Indeed, etc., and niche sites like InHerSight and FairyGodBoss, to name but a few. Google For Jobs also attaches reviews to search results in all North American and Latin American and Sub-Saharan African countries, 14 European countries, 15 Middle Eastern and North African countries, and 16 Asian countries.[11] Besides review sites, there are countless threads on Reddit, including the aptly named Recruiting Hell subreddit, and colourful commentary on Blind.

Today, many people of all age groups are unafraid to write their opinions on LinkedIn, and the TikTok generation has little concern about sharing their thoughts on employer behaviour. In January 2024, Brittany Pietsch shared a recording of how she was fired from Cloudflare without adequate explanation – she asked for it multiple times – by a non-empathetic HR who didn't even include her manager in the meeting. The video has gone viral; her manager was unaware of her layoff; the CEO's response has proven unpopular; the incident is now in media publications, and whether you agree with her actions or not, like Wayfair (in Chapter 1), it will cost Cloudflare future employees and, importantly, customers.

Sarah White and Tami Nutt, industry analysts at Aspect 43, have created a free guide and excellent reminder on how to lay off people ethically. For the sake of your people and the company's reputation, download a copy here: bit.ly/EthicalLayoffs (case sensitive).[12] Also, read Sue Ingram's book, *Fire Well: How to Fire Staff So They Thank You.*[13]

Of course, it is possible that your consumer brand might attract people, but if they run a search online and don't like what employees or applicants are saying, they won't apply. The internet opened the door to your company. If the employee or candidate experience is poor, people will discuss it online, costing you new hires, employees, and even sales.

Incorrect: Resumes Are the Determining Factor

> *It is untrue that a great resume guarantees a great hire, and inversely, a poorly written resume doesn't mean they are likely to be underperforming compared to their peers.*
> —Dirk Spencer, Tech Sector, USA
>
> *It's frustrating when managers think the resume tells the whole story or they feel justified rejecting a candidate because they think that if someone is interested in working for them, they will write a cutting-edge resume. . . after we approached them about the job!*
> —Tammy Bailey, Food & Beverage, USA

How easy do you find writing your own resume? There are so many questions that arise. What do you add? How do you write confidently without coming across as an egotistical know-it-all? What format or font do you use? Is it still OK to use bullets? Looking online doesn't make it easier when an internet search for 'how to write a resume' delivers 4 million results and template examples I know recruiters find hard to read. Paying for advice from resume writers is often expensive, conflicting, and sometimes outright untrue – for example, nobody needs an ATS-compliant resume!

When companies brutally slashed their talent acquisition teams in 2020, I noticed that most job-seeking recruiters had, ironically, poorly completed LinkedIn profiles and uninspiring CVs. If the people who spend their days looking at profiles and resumes find it hard to express their skills, expertise, and experience in a refined document or profile, it is little wonder that non-recruiters struggle.

Over on Threads, user @allaboutdogs_youtube, shared that she has been on the job hunt for six months, applied to 60 jobs, and had finally had someone approach her about a job. She had one interview and got the job.[14] Of course, I haven't seen her resume, so I am making an educated guess, but that one interview led to an offer epitomises the flaw in all hiring: great people are missed by companies due to the reliance on a document that is very difficult to create.

Unless you are recruiting an editor, writer, copywriter, etc., try not to dismiss resumes out of turn. Any talent acquisition partner worth their weight in gold will have seen past the document and conducted a thorough screening interview to determine if the person is worthy of proceeding. Instead of judging the applicant's ability to write or update their resume, trust the judgement of your talent acquisition partner, especially if you participated in a thorough recruitment alignment meeting and they actively sourced the applicant.

Untrue: Long Hiring Processes Ensure the Best Hire

> *Asking someone to jump through an unnecessarily long interview process does not prove their value and delivers a poor candidate experience. It also paints a negative picture about the manager's leadership style and the company culture.*
> —Aoife Brady, Human Services, Australia

On the subreddit mentioned earlier, Recruiting Hell, which provides an equal blend of amusement and horror, people share their experiences with companies and hiring processes. One of the most frequent complaints is about unduly long recruiting processes, and it is always interesting to read about those who chose to withdraw from them. Having an exceedingly long process makes it more likely to hire someone who tolerated the hoop-jumping, didn't get an alternate offer during the process, and is not necessarily the best person for the role.

In January 2024, Lauren Baer shared on LinkedIn:

I withdrew my candidacy recently from a company I REALLY liked. A company where I had interviewed with five different team members, including the CEO. All of them agreed I was, and I quote, "the strongest candidate". The CEO said they were down to two people. But at the last minute, they wanted me to complete another writing exercise. On top of the two I had already done, and they had already liked. It wasn't thought out, it was ill-defined, and the parameters meant it wasn't equitable if multiple candidates were tasked with it. It had me questioning whether they knew what they were looking for. Whether this was symptomatic of a bigger internal problem. Even their ethics. So I withdrew. Today, I saw the job listing was reposted. So either I was the only candidate all along, or the other person withdrew too.[15]

This post is the perfect example of a candidate concerned that interview inconsistencies indicate deeper issues, like the blame culture I mentioned in Chapter 1. Interestingly, Lauren only has a few thousand followers, but the post has evoked 56,000 reactions, 1700 comments and 777 reposts; thank goodness she didn't mention the company by name. Throughout the comments, many shared similar stories, congratulated her for knowing her worth, thought she dodged a bullet and believed the company didn't know what they were doing.

Misstep: Make People Wait

> *It surprises me that managers, who also receive many approaches about jobs, think that candidates will wait patiently for a response, even for weeks. They won't because it is easy to interview online, so they do that instead of waiting for any company's reply.*
> —Mohammed Karim Al Damen, Automotive, Kuwait
>
> *It's naive to think this is the only golden opportunity and that candidates will wait for an interview; they won't!*
> —Pratima Prasad, Food & Beverage, Australia

Consider the difference between not knowing when the train or bus will arrive, compared to the certainty of knowing exactly when it is due. Then, think about how amazing it is to be able to track a pizza delivery on an app. In contrast, what about the last time you sent an email, and someone didn't reply promptly or at all. Or worse, when you can see someone has read your message, yet you are still waiting for a reply. Ah, the emotions!

In a world that has become faster and with technology that revolves around the instant gratification of notifications, waiting has become frustrating. People expect swift responses and clarity; this includes their job application. They want transparency, to understand the process, and for people to respect their irreplaceable time. If you want to recruit the best person for the role, don't leave them hanging!

Fail: Talent Acquisition Doesn't Need Our Help

> *It's bad when hiring managers think they don't need to partner – that they can just be a passenger – like we are ordering a product from Amazon.*
> —Gail Sampson, Tech Sector, UK
>
> *Hiring requires joint accountability, managers need to partner with Talent Acquisition, just like they partner with HRBPs for retention.*
> —Mrinal Das, Telecommunications, India

By the end of this book, you will know many small things you can do to improve the whole process for everyone while saving yourself time, money, and face. You may also wish you had partnered with your talent acquisition team sooner!

Fallacy: Hiring Someone New Is the Only Answer

> *Recruiting isn't the answer to every problem. Finding more people won't fix a bad hiring process, won't fix a low salary budget, won't fix a 'requirements versus market' mismatch. It definitely won't fix turnover!*
> —Shawna Armstrong, Construction, USA

> *Consulting firm McKinsey found that 75% of executives think they can gain half of the skills required in the future from internal upskilling, not external hires. Yet, The World Economic Forum's Future of Jobs report states that only 41% of workers globally complete training that effectively bridges the skills gap; it is time to change that!*
>
> —Maud Durand, Tech Sector, UK

If talent acquisition professionals are permitted the time and resources to develop the function fully, they can work closely with HR and Learning & Development to identify any flight risks and potential internal candidates. They can also advise on the market salary for roles. Then, they can also align with workforce planning to identify if hiring anyone new is the correct decision.

Today, thanks to technology like plug-and-play WORQDRIVE, you can automate your workforce redeployment and talent mobility. When the cost of losing a salaried worker costs a company between 20 to 50% of their annual salary, considering redeployment, not a new hire or layoffs, should be high on the agenda.[16] But people will neither stay nor join if your company's culture is poor, so be sure to address this, too.

Recruiter Speak

One of the most significant issues I have witnessed is recruiter versus business jargon. It sometimes seems like you speak two different languages.

Let me start with one I would like recruiters to stop using. You may have noticed that I have only called you managers and leaders, not referred to you as hiring managers. I have intentionally done this because hiring is only a tiny part of your job and 100% of a recruiter's job. But mostly, I would like them to refrain from using this term because you are not managing the hiring process. It is either a joint effort or Talent Acquisition's job to manage the process. I would like you to be their hiring partner.

Some more jargon.

Job brief, kick-off or intake meeting	The call to discuss the role and hiring process. The recruitment alignment meeting that makes or breaks the entire process.
Talent Acquisition	The team involved in sourcing, advertising, hiring processes, onboarding, training, market mapping, managing the process, etc., i.e. more than just recruiting. They can also be involved in strategy and planning.
Recruiter	360° recruiters are usually only responsible for sourcing, interviewing, hiring, and, maybe, onboarding.
Talent or Recruitment Sourcer	Specialists in finding targeted prospects. They might contact these prospects; they may only research on behalf of a recruiter.
Prospect	Someone identified as a potential fit for a role but may not have been contacted yet.
Candidate	Someone who has been contacted and is interested in hearing more about the role. The term candidate is often misused for other parts of the hiring process.
Applicant	Someone who applied for the role in response to a job advertisement, an agency approach, or after contact from someone in Talent Acquisition.

Interviewee	Someone who has had a pre-screening call or is in the interview loop.
Candidate experience	The experience people have with a potential employer. A lousy one makes future hiring difficult.
Recruitment marketing	A targeted marketing strategy to entice, engage, and nurture people to apply to work for your company.
Employer brand	Where your consumer brand is for customers and clients, your employer brand is for future employees.
Job description	Best created in unison with the recruiter, it outlines the role's essential responsibilities and requirements.
Job advertise-ment or post	It should be like Coca-Cola is advertised, but too often, it is like someone listing the ingredients.

Reboot Your Relationship with Talent Acquisition

I called this book *Reboot Hiring* because I believe that, even when hiring is in flux, you can make recruitment easier if you reset your current approach: giving more time and consideration upfront so you waste less time down the line. It's about reconsidering a process and not about turning your talent acquisition team off and back on! Inert and staid are the last things you want to be to successfully attract, engage, and hire in this candidate-driven market, which it will remain as long as there is an internet. As trusted peers, you must partner closely with your talent acquisition professional to hire successfully.

Talent Acquisition Is Not Your Pawn

And you are not their Queen. You are not their client. You are their colleague. Talent Acquisition is not there to accept whatever outdated job brief you send their way or the endless list of must-haves. Nor do they exist to constantly rearrange interviews to suit last-minute schedule changes at the expense of the recruitment process and experience. They are not CV shufflers, administrators, or diary managers. Whether you are in the C-suite or a new manager, it is time to reboot your current perception of the power balance. To save time, money, and hassle when hiring, you must treat each other as equals, shoulder to shoulder, working together to fill the role.

As mentioned in Chapter 1, you must accept that your expertise falls in whatever it is you do and that their expertise is in finding, marketing, engaging, wooing, interviewing, qualifying, guiding, assuring, closing (or rejecting), and even onboarding the people who will join your team, now or in the future. The best recruiters will tell you when you are not being realistic, and they will provide the evidence to back it up. They will challenge you when you do things to sabotage the hiring process because they know that it will waste your time and the company's money and harm candidate experience and future hiring.

Commit

I get it; recruiting a member for your team is critical and a chore that quickly loses consideration during the daily routine. You need someone, but it is hard to prioritise because it is probably your most disliked task, and you are under the pressure created by being down a team member. But – and it is a big 'but' – when you are busy, you must make the time and, more importantly, commit to your side of the deal. Once you do, you will find that recruiting becomes less of a chore. Talent Acquisition does not want to waste your time any more than they want to waste their or the candidate's irreplaceable time.

Communicate

Chatting with one of the talent acquisition professionals in my mentoring group; he was venting his frustration at being unable to reach the manager. 'What have you tried?' I asked. 'Slack.' he replied, 'I have sent him about ten messages, all on Slack.' Countering, I suggested that maybe this manager doesn't like Slack and that he might prefer a phone call, an email, a text, or even an Instagram DM. OK, probably not the last one, but there are so many ways to communicate in 2024 that it is crucial to agree on how you will communicate and in what timeframe.

If your company has an applicant tracking system (ATS), I can guarantee that your recruiters will want you to use it proactively. You may have valid reasons for avoiding it, but using it for data protection and candidate experience reasons is wise. That said – recruiters won't appreciate me saying this – if you know you won't use it, just tell them! It is better to agree on how you like to communicate upfront so they can adapt to your style. But don't then ignore them when they contact you on your preferred channel; they are working with you, not against you, to fill the role.

Trust

When I tell people outside of the talent acquisition profession that I work with companies to help them fix recruitment and candidate experience, every single one of them tells me a recruitment horror story. You probably have one, too. That time you had your irreplaceable time wasted, or when you were ghosted, or worse. Like our opinions of our politicians, people hold strong feelings towards recruiters.

But don't let a previous experience jade your working relationship with your talent acquisition colleagues. Be honest with them about your past experiences and what you liked and didn't. Also, ask them about theirs. You may be surprised how poorly recruiters can treat other recruiters, and you will probably discover some common ground and a lot of empathy.

Once you have aired your concerns and agreed to a level of mutual respect, it will be easier to start trusting each other. It's essential to saving time, money, and face and having a more effective hiring process. Trust your talent acquisition partner to have correctly screened applicants. Trust their judgement to see beyond the words on the resume. And definitely aim to get to the point where you trust them when they insist you interview someone!

Share More

The more you help your recruiter understand what your team does and how that fits into the company's mission, the easier it will be for them to find and attract the right people to your roles. As much as you don't know the ins and outs of working in Talent Acquisition, they don't know how to do the job of the person you are hiring, so demystify it. Spend some time upfront explaining more, let them meet your team and hear from them, and be sure to answer any questions with compassion if they get confused.

Chapter Summary

- The internet opens the door to your company. It reveals the ways in which people are treated as employees or candidates in the hiring process, both positively and negatively.

- Talent Acquisition might be a relatively new department, but when given the opportunity by company leaders, it becomes your true partner in hiring the people your company needs to succeed now and in the future.

- Rather than continue misconceptions and power imbalances, managers and recruiters must create trusted, committed, honest, and communicative partnerships to reboot hiring.

- If you want to save time, money, and the potential embarrassment of a failed project or hire, invest a little more time at the start, using the formula I will outline on the following pages.

3

Let Talent Acquisition Thrive

What's your recruitment horror story? What specifically made it so bad that you still remember it? Did you learn something from the incident? Whatever it was, it is crucial not to let it jade your current hiring activities. You must let it go if you hope to create respectful partnerships with talent acquisition and recruiters and if you want to save time, money, and hassle when hiring.

Many years ago, I was at a party with my now ex-husband and innocently told someone I met that I was a technical recruitment consultant. It was like a red flag to a bull; he let rip with all his pent-up frustration about how unprofessional and money-hungry *all* IT recruitment consultants are. Strangely, I was pretty calm, but Richard changed colour with indignation on my behalf, like when a cartoon character goes red, filling up from foot to head with anger. Thankfully, the man moved on and has probably long forgotten the whole thing; I have not.

This poor perception of recruiters is something I work to change through my book, *The Robot-Proof Recruiter*, and my work. As with all professions, great and not-so-good people work in agency recruitment and internal talent acquisition. In my experience, much of the poor behaviour – on both sides – is due to a lack of training and investment.

In my 21 years, I have met two people who chose a career in recruitment; the vast majority fall into it. Unlike the HR profession, talent acquisition doesn't have a body as strong as the Society for Human Resource Management or the Chartered Institute of Personnel and Development, offering globally recognised qualifications. People often learn on the job, so the calibre varies greatly. When many talent acquisition teams are underfunded and under-resourced, it's a self-fulfilling prophecy.

As you heard, I fell into recruitment when I moved to London, UK, from Sydney, Australia, in 2003, after seeing an advertisement in a newspaper for a trainee recruitment consultant. The first two agencies, one with a severe cash-flow issue and one full of cowboys, were not for me, but they led me to Best, which became Spring Technology.

I was placed there by Tina Maddock, one of the finest recruiters-for-recruiters I have encountered; unknowingly, she showed me the importance of treating candidates with kindness, care, and compassion. At Best, I was trained by Steve Simms, Richard Norris, and Mel Agostini on every-thing involved in delivering a human-centred recruitment experience. They instilled in me that both clients and can-didates mattered, and by starting in the profession much later than most, I understood my impact on people's lives and livelihoods.

I'm sure some people might say I didn't treat them well, and there is that one interviewee I didn't give feed-back to when I worked in-house, which I still feel bad about. Overall, though, I chose to treat candidates and contrac-tors as I would like to be treated, which led to some heated conversations with Finance if they missed paying one of them, but I gained contractor loyalty. The true testament to how I treated them is that many are still friends today, over 18 years later, and they would have defended me from the furious man at the party. I don't say this to boast; I'm far from perfect. I say it because, to quote Maya Angelou, 'people never forget how you made them feel.'

Isn't it just common sense? Isn't it just manners? Weren't we raised to treat others how we would like to be treated? Yet people hide behind technology, not replying, disrespecting others, and often not thinking much of it. 'Oh, I was [insert a lame excuse].'

I'm pretty confident and happy after healing self-hate created through childhood trauma, but a recent experience of ghosting rattled my cage. I talked with two people about speaking at an event after their colleague referred me to them. I was firm when I said I would not do it for "exposure" because I have earned my stripes, and it is not a currency that pays bills. However, I emailed them both the next day with a name suggestion because this person would find this audience beneficial. No reply. A few days later, I tried again. No reply. Tried via a message on LinkedIn. No reply. I chased the referrer; she was as unimpressed as I was.

I kept replaying the conversation over and over in my head, creating self-doubt. Yes, of course, I had been Australian and spoken directly. Did they seem upset? Well, no, but then people mask. Hmm, maybe I shouldn't have commented on the lack of diversity. Oh, well, it is true. Then, the indignation hit. I am well-revered on the speaking circuit; don't they know I know all their other speakers? And on it went. Though other great client work was dropping in, the lack of response bugged me.

A month later, one of them replied, full of apology, horrified I felt ghosted, and with a valid excuse for the extended silence. Though I empathised, I had emailed two people; why didn't the other reply in their absence?

Horror Stories Must End

In an age where phones, usually within reach, are seldom phones but devices to access email, messages, and texts readily, communication should be straightforward. Yet, somehow, it has become challenging to connect and acceptable to ghost people. But, as I will keep reminding you, if you or your talent acquisition partner make someone feel less than impressed, the experience will end up online, visible to others.

This review is from a senior executive who interviewed at The Athletic in 2023:

> *I applied online and didn't hear back for over a month. Someone referred me, and I then heard back immediately. The recruiter was really not good and soured me on the whole process. He would not follow up for weeks at a time while still insisting I was their top candidate. He missed updating me about multiple things, and I was left guessing what was happening, when, and with whom. Ultimately, I saw it as a negative sign that a company didn't care about treating a so-called "top" candidate with even basic respect and withdrew from the process. Quite a shame, really, as I thought the company, their product, and the leadership team were all fantastic.*[1]

The concern is that this applicant was a referral, and one person's behaviour led to the executive withdrawing their application. So, like with my contact who referred me to the speaking work, both parties will have become annoyed. And worse, the managers and leaders lost a great applicant and may have had to start over. This recruiter might be incompetent; it would be easy to blame them for this incident, but it hints at something else.

So, let me play devil's advocate for a moment:

- 'I applied online and didn't hear back for a month' could mean that the recruiter had many applicants or was working on too many roles at once without proper support.
- 'Someone referred me, and I then heard back immediately' might infer that the applicant was in a pile with many others or that the recruiter was simultaneously working on too many roles.

- 'Would not follow up for weeks at a time' indicates the recruiter is unlikely to have an applicant tracking system or a good relationship with managers.
- 'Missed updating me about multiple things' again suggests that the recruiter is unlikely to have an ATS or a great relationship with managers and is probably over capacity, too.

To know for sure, we need more evidence. It is too easy to blame the recruiter when, in my experience, there are usually many reasons that talent acquisition professionals aren't thriving.

The Elephants in the Room

The communication and collaboration issues, the unsuitable technology, and Talent Acquisition being underfunded and underinvested in all come down to poor perception: the elephants in the room. Allow me to offer some alternative views based on my work with clients globally over twenty years and through more ups and downs than I care to remember.

Power Sits with Employees and Candidates

In some professions and countries, the economy or technology has shaken things up and made some companies feel like they are back in charge. But overall, with the visibility of jobs online and the ease of jumping onto a video interview, the choice remains firmly with employees and job seekers. They don't have to stay with you or choose you.

Job seeking in 2024 is different from in 1991 when I went on the hunt for my first job. Looking in a newspaper, where you couldn't see if other jobs were available or do anything but work within a commutable distance of the office, is poles apart from today. If someone had told me just 18 years later I would start working primarily from home, when it suits me, delivering to clients worldwide, I am not sure I would have believed them. Yet, I left the corporate hustle and created my destiny over the last nearly 15 years.

Working remotely in 2009 was more technologically challenging than in 2020, when all the companies that said their people couldn't possibly work remotely were forced to find ways to make it happen. Though I knew that the internet shifted employment choice from the company to people, I didn't predict so many knowledge workers refusing to return to arduous and polluting commutes and open-plan offices designed for extroverts. Even now, with mandated returns by some companies, people are still in charge.

Director of Technology Transformation Rachel Botts shared an insightful observation about remote work in the comments on a LinkedIn poll:

> There is an influx of opportunity for fully remote work with international companies who genuinely do not care where you sit when you do your work. There's a lot of talk about a reversal in trends. I have a handful of friends who already started this by relocating to teach English 20 years ago; now, even more, are working remotely in diverse sectors. I even see people move to the Caribbean with its low cost of living and working remotely for companies throughout Europe. It won't always be an employer's market here in the States if our companies don't meet workers' needs.[2]

Sharing his arduous job seeker experience during 2023, Director of Talent Acquisition David Bach raised a vital point:

Organisations must resist being lulled by short-term market dynamics. When employers feel the balance has shifted to an employer market, candidate experience goes out the window; this destroys employer reputation and creates future challenges of attracting talent as the cycle shifts back to an employee-driven market. The world of talent acquisition stands at a critical inflexion point, and a genuine evaluation is due. As we journey forward, it's essential to remember that talent acquisition isn't about slots and vacancies. It's about people, their aspirations, and their worth.[3]

Perceiving TA as a Cost Centre Is Costly

Accounting pedantry aside, humour me; consider the possibility that Talent Acquisition is anything but a cost centre. Because surely, it's too simple to consider the people who hire the people – the people that make the company succeed – as just a cost on a spreadsheet. Yet, as evidenced over the last four years, with the way talent acquisition teams are slashed, rehired, and slashed, it appears so. But let me proffer an alternative point of view, with a few examples.

Productivity: Star Hires Heidi Wassini, a Danish Talent Acquisition and Employer Branding Evangelist, transformed an outdated hiring process that Telenor's Head of Sales claimed increased store sales by 50% across Denmark. Realising their current hiring method wouldn't work, she introduced an assessment tool from AON. With the manager, she tested Telenor Denmark's top sales performers, which gave them a guide on who to hire. Then, they used the gamified 10-minute test instead of resumes and education, which showed a clearer picture of who to progress to a competency-based interview. The result of Heidi's proactivity was an efficient process that saved the managers time, money, and hassle, where all candidates received feedback – important when they could also be clients – and aided the company's bottom line.

Sophie Power, a British Talent Acquisition Lead, was tasked to find a mission-critical Electrical Components Sourcing Specialist to enable her company's expansion into the US. The successful candidate needed native-level fluency in English and Mandarin, an understanding of the local culture to source and negotiate successfully, and a willingness to travel quarterly to Shenzen. Not only did Sophie find, attract, and convert someone with this unique skill set, but the candidate was a woman, which helped with perspective on the company's FemTech products. The company has since successfully expanded into the US.

Saving: Agency Spend   Clive Smart is a British Head of Talent Acquisition at Moneysupermarket Group, a company of 630 employees. He shared, 'We've reduced agency spend by circa £500K in nine consecutive months with zero agency hires. The plan for 2024 is to work with only a small number of agency partners who will fill 5% or fewer of roles.' When I asked if managers also save time because they're conducting fewer interviews, he said, 'It is always better for managers when talent acquisition finds the candidates because we understand the role, team and environment better, so can make better matches.'

When US Talent Acquisition Leader Adam Meekhof took over one department at a company of 800 employees, within 12 months, he and the team cut the recruitment agency spending by $2.7 million. He took control of the agencies back from managers, reducing the number from 20 to 3 and the percentages from as high as 40% to a more acceptable 20–22%. He said, 'On day 1, we had 135 open roles; by the end of the year, it was 5. We also backfilled about 45 roles. It shows what a high calibre talent acquisition team can achieve for a company; they were incredible.'

Saving: Transformation Global HR and Talent Leader Jo Menon has over 20 years of experience in HR change programme management, including global rollouts of new or upgraded HRIS and TA systems. Jo steps in when HR or the IT project management office is light on HR-specific programme or change management expertise. For example, she led the implementation of a new applicant tracking system across 115 countries for IWG PLC, formerly Regus, which included building online employment contracts and automated onboarding in multiple languages.

Jo said:

> *It was complex, but we delivered on time and to budget. The key that ensured managers' and leaders' buy-in to the new applicant tracking system was including them in non-time-consuming testing. Hence, they understood the investment and experienced the benefits the system would make in their daily working lives. The ROI was significant, including cost and time savings from improved process automation, reduced process steps, quicker response times and a better user experience by removing most of the manual communication between recruiters, managers and candidates, and fast clear talent acquisition reporting.*

Saving: Retention Thirty per cent of new hires leave within 90 days; 43% because the role didn't meet expectations; 34% because of a specific incident; 32% found the company culture wasn't a fit.[4] However, this is far less likely to happen when managers and leaders partner with and respect Talent Acquisition and know who they need to hire.

Amy Miller directly recruits engineers and space lab technicians for Amazon's Project Kuiper and said in a LinkedIn post: 'I don't think retention should be a recruiting metric, but I'm damn proud that most of the folks I've hired in the last four years are still here – many of them one or two levels above where we started.'[5] Amy's relationship with her managers and leaders sets recruitment up for success and means they don't waste time, large sums of money, and suffer hassle rehiring for each role.

Saving: Avoiding Bad Hires   In my in-house role, I successfully recruited the niche IT consultants required to deliver essential client projects. However, without my input, the person responsible for the sales to date hired a Sales Director so he could promote himself to COO. I immediately knew this person wasn't right but had been excluded from the entire recruitment process, and my concerns fell on deaf ears. The new hire didn't make sales, current client work wasn't extended, the bench started filling up with consultants, and later, thankfully, after I had departed, the company imploded. A broader and fair hiring process facilitated by Talent Acquisition could have prevented this outcome.

Over the years, I have lost count of the number of talent acquisition specialists who have told me that they only gained the respect of their manager when they ignored their concerns over an interviewee. Instead of trusting in their experience initially, the managers went ahead with the hire, only to have it fail.

According to the US Department of Labor, a bad hire costs 30% of the employee's first-year earnings; other sources cite figures from $17,000 to a staggering $240,000.[6,7] Unsurprising when you include the cost of lost productivity for you and the team, the potential to lose clients or damage the relationship, the time wasted supervising the poor hire, training costs, legal or even severance fees, etc. To calculate yours, try the bad hire calculator created by GrassGreener Group at bit.ly/bhcalculator.

Yet, poor hires are avoidable. When Talent Acquisition is appropriately funded, trained, and respected, it can implement a fair and equitable hiring process and help you articulate who you need so you avoid bad hires.

Saving: New Hires According to research from BambooHR, 29% of new starters know in the first week if the job is a fit, and 44% of employees say they have had regrets or doubts about accepting the job within the first week.[8] And as I demonstrate through this book, this is preventable.

Onboarding is the critical point where Talent Acquisition hands the hiring process to HR or the manager to prepare for the new hire's start. In my opinion, asking Talent Acquisition to own onboarding isn't a wise use of their skills, but according to my LinkedIn poll, 19% of respondents are actively involved in onboarding. However, 7% get involved to keep it smooth, and 47% watch closely to ensure it happens. Leaving just 28% confident that the candidate they offered will receive a great onboarding experience.[9]

Danielle Morgan shared on Threads, 'My worst onboarding experience at a new job: my boss didn't turn up, no training, and no direction or insight into what they wanted me to do.' In the comments, Annie Ko added one I see far too frequently: 'I didn't have a laptop the 1–2 weeks I started, and my boss was out of the country. I just sat there.'[10]

Companies with an onboarding programme retain 58% of employees for three years, and 77% of new hires hit their first performance milestone.[11] Don't undermine Talent Acquisition's work and waste your time rehiring due to a messy and ultimately expensive onboarding experience. And please ensure they receive their tech!

Denied Technology Efficiencies

In 2018, when I was approached about writing a book, I immediately knew what I wanted to write about: the myth that robots will replace recruiters. Even now, in 2024, I don't believe they are replaceable by AI or any other technology, but talent acquisition needs it to do their jobs effectively. Yet they are refused it too frequently; many are left begging for more than a basic applicant tracking system.

Not giving Talent Acquisition the tools they need is short-sighted when candidate behaviour is not dissimilar to consumer behaviour; they expect a smooth, transparent, and friendly process, or they withdraw or don't apply. The right technology in the right place is essential for delivering a candidate experience that is talked about online for all the right reasons. Plus, ultimately, it will save you time, money, and hassle.

Talent Acquisition needs technology that helps with finding, engaging, communicating, transparency, building pools, reminders, scheduling, and more. Just like your Marketing and Sales teams, they need a combination of tools to do their jobs efficiently and effectively.

On top of a fit-for-purpose applicant tracking system – not an unfit HRIS add-on! – they will want to add sourcing technology for swiftly locating and contacting suitable prospects, recruitment-specific marketing platforms to engage and re-engage candidates and build pools of interested parties, interview and assessment technology, and onboarding tools to ensure people start well.

Be Wary of Snake Oil   Many HR tech vendors claim to be able to fix recruitment; some even believe recruiters are replaceable. Having read this far, hopefully, you are no longer one of them because more technology isn't the answer to fixing the main issues preventing great hiring: communication and collaboration. Mobile phones are evidence of how technology has made communication harder due to the overwhelming number of channels and the ease of "getting back to people later", leading to ignoring or ghosting people, intentionally or not. Neglected databases are more evidence that having technology doesn't mean people will use it to share information with their colleagues.

The HR tech landscape is vast and confusing. I regularly receive pitches from HR tech vendors who claim to have the answer to every talent acquisition problem, yet on inspection, they don't. Often, these creations are from people who have never worked as a recruiter but somehow think they know what is needed. Perhaps that would be okay for technology that supports sales professionals selling a product that doesn't have thoughts, feelings, and emotions and goes where it is told, but it's unacceptable for talent acquisition.

Remember the HRIS add-on ATS I mentioned in Chapter 2 that led to more work, not less? Costly errors happen when technology buyers and decision-makers have never been recruiters or don't respect the team's input, or someone falls for the snake oil because they are overworked, under-resourced, and desperate for something to alleviate the pain. In *The Robot-Proof Recruiter*, I encourage talent acquisition professionals to get recommendations from their peers and only purchase technology that is proven to save everyone – managers, recruiters, and candidates – time and hassle. Only implement technology designed by or with the input of recruiters who understand the complexity of the process and how to deliver an employer brand-boosting candidate experience.

Communities your talent acquisition team can seek peer advice from include (TTC) The Talent Community, IHR's LinkedIn group or Slack channel, and Higher Community.[12,13,14]

The False Economy of Firing the TA Team

Watching entire talent acquisition teams fired in 2020 was heart-breaking, but I could almost understand it as I, too, fought to keep my doors open. Then, in 2021, I witnessed companies frantically trying to reestablish the function as soon as they needed to hire. For the first time in my career, recruiters were unicorns, and they knew it, but they dove back in and gave their all, helping companies get back on track. But then, from mid-2022 to late 2023, I watched entire teams fired again as too many companies realised they had not planned properly and had massively overhired. In 2024, I see companies hiring talent acquisition professionals again as the market finally seems to be rebalancing.

Perhaps you think it makes sense that the company should fire the recruiters if you're not hiring. But consider these five costs created by this rollercoaster behaviour.

Communication Breakdown   If cutting the talent acquisition team does not indicate an overall company hiring freeze and recruiters are locked out of their systems immediately, consideration must be made about who takes over candidate communication, if that's still possible. Zealous IT departments that think laid-off employees will become a threat create havoc for candidates, managers, and leaders and affect employee morale.

Former Sourcing Recruiter at Amazon Web Services Michael Zuino shared in a post on LinkedIn in early 2023:

> *One of the many downfalls of these immediate layoffs are impacts to those in the interview process. I've just had a candidate reach out to me because their contact for their interview was laid off. I had to let them know I was also laid off, but this candidate, on what should be a big day, is left scrambling and stressed out.*[15]

Further on, Michael added:

It pains me not to be able to help them. I've read about countless recruiters who were let go when they had a candidate at the offer stage. I have projects that I was working on. My peers have projects that they are working on as well. And then, once you're laid off, that's it. You're locked out, and all the work you were doing, unless you had the foresight to send it to somebody else, is gone. I understand why layoffs are often immediate, but this gives no time for people to wrap up loose ends, share their work, and provide our customers [candidates] the experience they deserve.

I can only imagine how many candidates withdrew from the process due to this instability, and I wonder how many were AWS customers, too.

Lost Pipeline Without Talent Acquisition, who will keep the people interested in working for your company engaged until you start recruiting again? Nobody. Everyone else is busy.

Losing the talent pipeline is a costly mistake in sectors where people have their choice of jobs. Instead of having a warm pool of people to recruit from, the company will start cold, adding to the cost and time required to hire and the knock-on impact on deliverables and deadlines. In hiring freezes, the talent acquisition team can be market mapping, building the talent pipeline, creating fresh content, and keeping people engaged, ready for the thaw.

Costly Inefficiencies Instead of turfing Talent Acquisition out, challenge them to streamline processes, cut vendor and supplier costs, and find efficiencies to pay for themselves first. Now they have some time away from day-to-day role-filling, they can complete neglected projects that will save the company time, money, and hassle in the future.

For example, they might be able to finally implement a better, less expensive applicant tracking system to deliver a finer candidate experience and improve the employer brand. What other legacy technology is costly, inefficient, and no longer fit for purpose? They will know.

Cost of Rehiring the TA Team   Adding to the expense that is outlaid laying off the team will be the cost of rehiring the team. Not just the fees for advertising or the agency but also the time consumed and hassle created to ensure you hire the right talent acquisition team; hiring great recruiters is as complex and vital as hiring great salespeople. Then there is the costly time required to integrate this new team: creating new partnerships with managers, understanding the culture and microcultures, learning the mission and values, reigniting the talent pipeline, mapping a new market, etc.

Cost-cutting when rebuilding a talent acquisition team is short-sighted, too. Though Barry Johnston was talking about agency recruiters in his LinkedIn article, 'Fire your recruiter: when it's time to rethink your hiring strategy', this matters for both sides: 'Inexperienced recruiters might not yet have the proficiency to recognise subtle red flags or the finesse to handle sensitive negotiations, which can result in a less-than-optimal hiring process. More importantly, they may lack the strategic foresight to devise a long-term hiring plan that aligns with your business objectives and market trends.'[16]

Over 2023, I have seen inexperienced people gaining senior management or director-level talent acquisition roles, where ageism and cost-cutting appear to be factors. Confidentially, a Global Talent Acquisition Leader currently hiring for a VP of People Operations, shared that two applicants in their fifties confessed in the interview that their leader was incompetent and didn't have the experience to learn from. When this team recruits the people for your company, you want a strong strategic leader who will develop the team into a world-class function. Hiring someone junior as a short-term cost-saving exercise could lead to the loss of valuable employees and long-term damage to the brand and productivity.

Damage to the Employer Brand In September 2023, Callie Hughes was laid off at 3 am on her honeymoon from her dream job as a recruiter for Google Cloud.[17] She shared this on LinkedIn, 'It's been a hard year for so many, but recruiters especially, as we navigated mass layoffs in the industry and our own companies, but kept our heads up, a smile on our face and continued to hire as demand still grew, expectations of us never changed, and hundreds of thousands of impacted people looked to us for help.' She added that she loved 'hiring people into their dream jobs all while doing and living mine'.

As you have read, layoffs can damage both the consumer and employer brand when conducted poorly. Laying off the talent acquisition team is no exception; they are the front door to employment at your company and know that reviews, even anonymous ones, make future hiring difficult. Surprisingly, talent acquisition is a niche profession; how employers treat people becomes visible across the network, even by old-school word of mouth, making hiring a new talent acquisition team challenging, slow and costly. Imagine how hard it is recruiting for Wayfair at the moment; picture being the recruiter trying to gush about a company with a 33% CEO approval on Glassdoor, poor press, and countless negative reviews.

You won't be on a hiring freeze forever; perhaps firing the talent acquisition team isn't the right move for the company's future.

Talent Acquisition Roles

Of course, the size of your talent acquisition team depends on your company's size. I also swiftly realised that distilling the typical roles into a few pages would be interesting. So, what follows is some gross generalising and grouping of titles, but it aims to spark some ideas and understanding.

Caveat: This is high-level material and not designed to be used as a job description. When hiring, it is better to use Chapter 4 to determine who you specifically need for your organisation.

Talent Acquisition Coordinators

Sometimes called recruitment coordinators, talent acquisition coordinators keep things moving through the hiring process and provide invaluable and essential administrative support for the rest of the team. They take the pressure off by focusing on tasks like writing job descriptions, preparing offer letters, benchmarking compensation, updating the database or applicant tracking system, performing background and reference checks, and coordinating interviews. They can also be involved in preparing reports and candidate experience surveys, organising the employee referral process, and even assisting with onboarding new hires.

Talent acquisition coordinators can benefit significantly from technology. For example, tools that help with scheduling, tracking, writing, and contract management are beneficial and could free them up to help improve the candidate experience.

Undoubtedly, coordinators are at the greatest risk from artificial intelligence. However, it's also an opportunity. Sophie Power, a Scotland-based talent acquisition professional, shared that 'AI allows coordinators to free up time to collaborate with marketing on employer brand initiatives, which is a great way to stretch and develop them and give candidates what they want. Also, training them in data analytics so they can drill data and provide insights will create more efficiencies in talent acquisition.'

If recruiting a talent acquisition coordinator, I would want them to demonstrate:

- Confident and excellent communication skills.
- Tenacity, determination, resilience, creativity and curiosity.
- A love of paperwork, being organised, and the importance of this role.
- Experience with an ATS or the tech-savvy to pick one up quickly.

Sourcers

Sometimes called talent sourcers or researchers, one thing sourcers are not is junior recruiters! That thinking definitely needs a reboot because they have a unique and refined set of skills. They are the hunters looking for people across the internet who could be a superb match for opportunities. Rather than just use LinkedIn, talented sourcers hone their skills at SourceCon or SOSU Sourcing Summits or read Jan Tegze's *Full Stack Recruiter* and will find people where they prefer to hang out.[18] They also know which of your company's competitors are great to target. Some just gather profiles, but most will make contact, match them to roles, and pass them to a talent acquisition specialist when the prospect is ready to apply.

In some larger companies, where similar roles recur regularly, sourcers work to create pools of interested people rather than working on a specific vacancy; they identify people who could be a match for more than one role or with more than one manager. Exceptional sourcers grow a steady stream of engaged prospects interested in joining your company when the opportunity arises. Sourcers love tools, especially technology, which helps them efficiently find, contact, and track prospects.

If I were hiring, I would want my sourcer to demonstrate:

- Curiosity, adaptability, resilience, flexibility, and a thirst for learning.
- Knowledge of finding and contacting people beyond LinkedIn.
- Tech-savvy skills, knowledge of tools, and persistence to navigate website changes.
- Passion for sourcing; it's not for everyone!

Talent Acquisition Specialists

Depending on the organisation, one could also call talent acquisition specialists, talent acquisition partners, business partners, advisors, consultants and more variations, conditional on seniority and duties. Usually, I would say that a 360° recruiter or in-house recruiter performed fewer duties, but researching for this section showed a lot of blurred lines.

So, for ease, I am grouping everyone who works in Talent Acquisition and is not a coordinator, sourcer, manager or director into this category.

Your talent acquisition professional should do all or some of the following: partner with managers or leaders on roles, help them articulate who they need, determine selection criteria, design job descriptions and interview questions, source potential candidates directly, via referrals or through advertising, assess applicant or prospect suitability, agree and schedule the interview stages, and conduct screenings or assessments. They could also be involved in employer branding initiatives, job fairs, and recruitment events, and forecasting needs in conjunction with HR business partners, workforce planning, or talent intelligence.

Like coordinators, specialists also benefit significantly from technology. They will also need tools to help with sourcing, scheduling, tracking, writing, interviewing, and general administrative tasks. Don't be surprised if they want to use technology to improve candidate communication and experience or employer brand; they should be well aware of the impact of social media and online reviews on recruitment.

In an interview, I would like a talent acquisition specialist to demonstrate the following:

- Curiosity, emotional intelligence, confidence, empathy, resilience, and flexibility.
- Where and how they challenge managers to ensure they hire who they need, not want.
- What they do to keep managers engaged and how they build trust and partnership.

- That they are more than administrators: ideas for improving talent acquisition for all.
- Data literacy and an aptitude for using it to tell stories and influence, and tech-savvy skills.

Talent Acquisition Managers

For ease again, I am grouping talent acquisition managers, heads of, and team leaders here. Depending on the level and your company size, the role may or may not involve actively partnering with managers or leaders on live job vacancies. Either way, they will have significant hands-on recruitment experience. In addition, they will be involved in determining current hiring needs and producing forecasts, developing strategies and hiring plans, and leading employer branding endeavours.

Great talent acquisition managers are adept at managing and influencing stakeholders and building authentic relationships with people across the business. They know how to communicate in different styles to lead effectively to create positive change and impact. They can develop innovative strategies and plans that meet organisational objectives and motivate the team to achieve them. They understand the importance of delivering a good candidate experience and its impact on the employer brand and future hiring, so they invest in and develop their team to be brilliant partners to managers and flourishing talent acquisition professionals.

When hiring, I'd want a talent acquisition manager to demonstrate the following:

- The ability to improve the perception of Talent Acquisition with leaders and the business.

- Vulnerability, owning mistakes, openness to feedback, approachability, and zero ego.
- Team support: protecting them from escalations when they are creating partnerships.
- How they motivated admin-style talent acquisition professionals to be proactive partners.
- Team development: through training, conferences and events, mentoring, books, etc.

On that last point, I delivered a webinar about sourcing to a director-level HR and Talent Acquisition group about eight years ago. At the end, one said in the proudest tone, 'My team doesn't have time to learn; they are maxed out.' What a disservice to the company! With training, the team could recruit better, more productive people, and they will be more likely to stay because they were invested in and grew. Ensure your talent acquisition leaders don't have a similar attitude.

Talent Acquisition Directors

I am grouping again; this time, I am calling talent acquisition directors, anyone in the function with an executive-level title or, possibly, those who may have management titles but play a strategic role and report directly to the CEO. Basically, those who establish and oversee the company's talent acquisition approach and collaborate with recruiters, hiring managers, and executives to achieve it. To succeed in leading a thriving function, they must be free of an active requirement load and have extensive experience and expertise to mould it.

Talent acquisition directors oversee all sourcing and hiring processes, ensure talent acquisition projects align with organisational objectives, cultivate a culture of excellence, and develop clear goals for the function. They also implement guidelines that ensure the company meets mandatory regulations and hiring and talent acquisition trends. They set and update executives on sourcing and hiring metrics and indicators. Like talent acquisition managers, they also facilitate training and programmes, liaise and negotiate with suppliers and vendors, and work to improve the candidate experience and employer brand.

When hiring one, I'd want the talent acquisition director to demonstrate the following:

- How they partnered with talent intelligence, workforce planning, and HR to reduce overhiring and improve retention through outstanding talent acquisition partnerships.
- How they motivated, supported, and developed an administrative function and transformed them into enterprising talent acquisition partners and proactive recruiters.
- Where and how they improved the perception of Talent Acquisition with managers and leaders, and its impact on attracting candidates, hiring metrics, and the bottom line.
- How they smoothed hiring processes and future-proofed the function through market mapping, talent pooling, employer branding, technology, upskilling, suppliers, etc.

In my experience, I have seen managers and directors carry out these duties; there is a lot of variance between organisations globally. Work out who your company needs in its Talent Acquisition function, and only take my attempt to describe these roles as a mere starting point.

Distinguishing Skills

While writing, a LinkedIn AI-generated collaborative article popped up in my feed, posing an interesting question: What are the most overlooked skills for getting promoted in Global Talent Acquisition?[19] Whether your Talent Acquisition is a global function or not, I felt the following snippets of people's answers were worth highlighting.

Sahana HS, a Senior Talent Acquisition Partner in India, added, 'The ability to adeptly navigate diverse cultural landscapes, showcasing cultural sensitivity, is highly prized.' Amira Said, a Global Talent Acquisition Leader in Egypt, stated: 'The most overlooked skills are cross-cultural communication, adaptability to diverse hiring practices, strategic thinking, and leveraging data analytics to optimise recruitment processes.'

Brian Miller, a VP of Talent Acquisition in the US, added, 'Emotional intelligence is vital for navigating stress and uncertainty; it aids in pressure management, feedback handling, and conflict resolution, fostering trust and rapport.' Similarly, Alexandra Davis, a Senior Recruiter in Sweden, shared, 'Emotional intelligence enables a deeper understanding of the human element behind data, fostering meaningful connections. Adaptability ensures resilience. Cross-cultural competence is crucial for effectively engaging with diverse talent pools and enhancing organisational inclusivity. Strategic foresight allows for anticipating future trends and aligning recruitment strategies for long-term success.'

All respondents mentioned strong manager or leader relationships, data literacy, project management skills, and business acumen. I was also relieved to see the emphasis on human skills in most replies because anyone who has worked in talent acquisition or recruitment knows recruiting people for other people is an emotional rollercoaster for all involved and takes grit and determination.

Other Significant Roles

Growing areas that can sit in talent acquisition or fall into wider HR include:

- **Employer Branding:** the people responsible for developing, managing, and delivering candidate attraction and engagement activities that improve the employer brand and attract more applicants and employees to the business.
- **Talent Intelligence:** the people using people analytics, sourcing intelligence, workforce planning, and labour market trends to inform a wiser talent acquisition strategy.
- **Talent Operations:** the people who track hiring metrics, suggest improvements, forecast future talent needs, and help Talent Acquisition operate more effectively and efficiently.

Flexible Alternatives

It is possible that your company does not have the hiring pipeline to justify having its own fully staffed Talent Acquisition function or is simply looking for another way. In that case, there are now alternatives to using a traditional recruitment agency or recruitment process outsourcing (RPO) company. The arrival of the internet allows everyone to reach the people who were tucked away in agency databases, and this reach has enabled new companies to offer flexible hiring models; here are some examples.

Talent Acquisition as a Service

Founded by Katrina Hutchinson-O'Neill, Join Talent is a TAaaS business that provides companies with the technology, people, and expertise required to hire, onboard, and manage the talent they need to meet their growth plans. They create bespoke solutions that give their clients expertise in building, shaping, and delivering on in-house talent attraction and retention. Their solutions are more agile and flexible than those of a traditional RPO.

Founded by Martin Dangerfield, immersive has been built to meet the challenges of talent acquisition leaders, filling the gaps in capacity and capability. They have worked across all organisation sizes but are perfect for growing SMEs where they manage the end-to-end hiring with an in-house team big enough to hire on a local, regional, and global basis and introduce all the processes, technology and data insight needed to succeed. They operate on an on-demand basis, handing back TA when hiring needs decline and ready to deploy when needed again. Recently, they have developed a consulting capability to optimise hiring processes, develop employee value proposition strategies, improve the candidate journey, and create inclusive, collaborative hiring experiences.

Talent Acquisition Project Managers

Perfect for fast-growth companies. Glenn Martin founded Never Mind The Job Spec, which creates bespoke hiring solutions for startups and scale-ups. Using a human-centred approach, they fuse positive candidate experience, talent brand advocacy, and values-based hiring to attract and engage diverse global talent. They act as the company's talent acquisition project partner, seamlessly melding with your team. They have successfully scaled companies from 3 to 80 new team members across multiple functions through human-centred hiring experiences that deliver dynamic, motivated, and engaged hires.

A Word of Caution   In my agency days, I suffered when my favourite client introduced an RPO. From being a sole supplier who met managers and the team, conducted proper recruitment alignment meetings, and knew who would fit because I walked the floors, suddenly, I was one of six, working off outdated, incoherent job descriptions and no longer permitted to speak to anyone but this new go-between. Unsurprisingly, I filled very few roles, prospects were frustrated by multiple agent approaches and thought less of the company, and managers hated it.

These days, most agency alternatives will work with very few staffing recruiters. However, whoever you choose to outsource to, to protect your employer brand, it is worth checking how they treat their suppliers.

Fractional TA Leader

This is a recent development in the world of talent acquisition, but it is worth mentioning because it is like having an expert on speed dial. A fractional TA leader can flexibly support inexperienced talent acquisition managers and directors with their wealth of experience. For example, founded by Kat Kingshott, Touchstone Talent offers fractional TA and consulting for specific projects such as candidate assessment, employer branding, diversity initiatives, ATS implementation, and streamlining the interview process, delivered on a subscription or project basis.

Chapter Summary

- Most recruiters fall into the profession and learn on the job; invest in them with training, events, conferences, books, coaching, and mentoring.
- Without the proper funding, resources, and technology, the function is set up to fail, which impacts employer and consumer brands, productivity, morale, and the bottom line.
- Treating Talent Acquisition as a cost centre overlooks its role in recruiting star hires, cutting costs of suppliers and through transformation, retaining employees, helping avoid bad hires, and ensuring new hires feel welcome.
- Reconsider knee-jerk termination of the entire talent acquisition team in a hiring freeze.
- Talent Acquisition includes coordinators, sourcers, specialists, managers, and directors.
- Thanks to the internet, new flexible alternatives and external support exist.

4

Articulating the Need

The costs associated with a bad hire have been identified in a Recruitment & Employment Confederation UK survey.[1] The top three costs are the time and money spent on training the employee (53%), the negative impact on employee morale and performance (46%), and the time and money spent in the hiring process (41%). These are closely followed by a general loss of productivity (36%), harm to the business's reputation (24%), financial loss (23%), and increased staff turnover (21%). It was also found that spending inadequate time reviewing the need, creating a misleading job profile, or focusing on competencies instead of potential were common mistakes leading to a bad hire.

Working out and successfully articulating who you genuinely need to recruit can be challenging. But getting it wrong is the crux of most failed recruitment, worsened if you don't have a strong talent acquisition partner to challenge assumptions and coax the information out of you. This chapter will help you explain to your hiring partner – to the best of your ability – who you need to hire to help you avoid these costs and so you also save time and hassle.

You might be a new manager who has never hired someone before and doesn't know where to start. You could be a senior leader who once believed "I'll know it when I see it" was an acceptable and fair way to hire but now wants to deliver a better experience for people. You might simply be too time-poor to give this extended thought and have defaulted to 'recruiting people like me', which isn't working.

When someone resigns, the thought pattern too often defaults to something like, 'Oh no, Jack's leaving! We need to replace Jack! Where's his job description? Call HR; they might have it. Oh, wait, here it is!' as a mouldy document is pulled from the dusty bottom drawer. 'Perfect, that'll do!' But it won't do; it is looking backwards. It overlooks that

Jack gained skills during his tenure with the company or that his current skills may not suit upcoming projects. Jack might need to be replaced by a Jill, and taking the time to figure out who you need to hire is essential before you invest time and energy in interviewing.

In this chapter, I will provide questions to help you challenge traditional thinking about job descriptions and ask you to consider market reality rather than media hype.

The Profile

From my network of high-calibre recruiters, I asked a few to share their favourite thought-provoking questions to get you started expressing who you need to hire. Grab a blank sheet of paper and start jotting down your immediate thoughts in response to these questions. Think of this as your shoddy first draft. It will be full of mistakes, but the idea is to look forward and find who you need, gather facts, and get curious about the person you need.

Who and What

Take a moment to clear some space. Take a deep breath – you may want to close your eyes – and picture yourself in 12 months. You are at your desk, and you are thinking about this person. You can see all the completed work and achievements; you know the qualities and behaviours they demonstrated. You wonder, 'What have they accomplished that makes me know for certain that I hired the right person?'

This question creates an easy way to come up with the "real" deliverables and the human qualities this person will need for the role because it quantifies your knowledge of the company and pipeline, the required expertise and experience, and the work they are coming in to complete. Your answer will be something along the lines of, 'I will know I hired the right person because they will have delivered_____ and have completed _____. And, thank goodness they have_____skills because they were needed [here] and [here]. Plus they will_____.'

For example, 'I will know I hired the right person because they will have delivered the new programme and have completed the implementation. And thank goodness they have excellent technical and communication skills because they were needed when communicating change to our leaders and employees. Plus, they created rapport with our clients, something lacking in their predecessor that cost us dearly when we lost a key client.'

American recruiter Steve Levy has decades of recruitment experience and suggests using these, too:

- *What work are you trying to accomplish that this recruit will help you achieve?*
- *What problems keep you awake at night that they can help resolve?*
- *What problems are you solving as a team, or what projects are you delivering?*

Similarly, American Talent Partner Jim Conti likes asking this tough one:

- *What have we failed at that they are coming in to fix?*

Curious about the desired character traits, Joanna Lubowicz, a Poland-based Senior Talent Acquisition Specialist, likes asking:

- *At work, who made a lifelong impression on you from the moment they started and why?*
- *If you could, who would you hire from your family for this and why?*

Joanna explained, 'I don't know why it works, but I have found that managers share the qualities of someone, and they end up being the qualities needed for the role. It's the same with the family question; they describe characteristics perfect for the role.'

For all these questions, if this new person will be a critical part of the team, get them involved. By answering the same questions, they might reveal something you have yet to consider. Plus, it will help them feel valued and invested in the new team member's success.

Success Profiles

German-based Talent, Organizational & Work Transformation Consultant Elizabeth Lembke was the first person I thought of when it came to this chapter because she specializes in all things related to talent and impact at work. Elizabeth also firmly believes you shouldn't hire someone unless you can keep them in a 20% downturn, but I digress. She shared the formula she uses to create Success Profiles for Critical Roles when working with her clients.

Step 1: Start with the following questions about the current and future challenges of the role (you may have some answers from the previous questions):

- *How does the role drive or support the strategy of the organisation?*
- *What are the expectations and deliverables?*

- *Which behaviours measurably impact key performance indicators?*
- *What differentiates high performers from average or low performers?*
- *What challenges will be faced internally and externally in the short and long term?*
- *What competencies do people in this role need to support the business effectively?*

Step 2: Define the competencies and traits necessary to succeed. Competencies are observable skills and behaviours required to succeed. They are evoked by a person's traits, which are the tendencies a person leans towards and include personality traits.

As you detail the competencies, check them with these questions:

- *Is this behaviour demonstrated by people who most effectively perform the work? That is, are people who don't demonstrate this behaviour ineffective in the role?*
- *Is this behaviour relevant and necessary for effective work performance?*
- *Is someone who excels in this competency more likely to be successful?*
- *Social or other competence gap: what would likely derail a career in your company?*
- *In the future of work, will this competency be a differentiator?*

Step 3: Define the experiences and drivers necessary to succeed. Experiences are assignments, positions, or jobs that prepare a person for future roles. Drivers are someone's values, interests, sense of unique contribution, motivation, and engagement.

- *What previous experiences are essential to setting this person up for success in this role?*
- *Does this role have leadership demands? If so, what kind?*
- *What background or qualifications can help someone jump-start in this role?*

Skill-Based Hiring

Over 2023, I witnessed the rise and push towards skill-based hiring, and I'll confess, I worried that someone could be highly skilled and toxic. My concern seems justified, too; a survey by Leadership IQ, tracking 20,000 hires over three years, revealed that 46% failed within their first 18 months – 89% for attitudinal reasons and just 11% for functional or technical skill causes. Keep this in mind when shifting to skill-based hiring.

The benefit of this method, though, is that moving away from credential-based hiring opens up a broader and more diverse talent pool, and it can aid retention. Instead of judging university degrees and other conventional certifications, the applicant's skills are assessed against those that lead to success in the role. It can also aid in reducing classism or elitism when deductions are made, for example, that those with degrees from the most privileged universities will outperform those with degrees from others. However, it is essential in the interview process not to reintroduce classism when making assumptions based on hearing someone's accent, for example.

Of course, there will always be roles where traditional qualifications are essential, but for many other roles, they are no guarantee of success. Traditionally, companies assess based on competencies, the knowledge, behaviours, attitudes, and skills that create the ability to do something well.

Meanwhile, according to Degreed, 'Skills are the learned and applied abilities that use one's knowledge effectively in execution or performance. Skills can be developed, can be measured, are applicable, and are transferable.'[2]

Quoting from McKinsey, *The Financial Times* article, 'Quiet hiring: Why managers are recruiting from their own ranks', shared that, 'One in 16 workers globally may have to switch occupations by 2030 as their roles become obsolete, and nearly nine in 10 executives say they face imminent skills gaps. Faced with the need for new and developing skills, many employers are choosing to retrain their own workers rather than recruit externally.'[3] This is excellent news for retention when lack of career advancement is the second reason most people resign; people want to learn and grow within a company.[4]

Though it is called skill-based hiring, it flourishes when implemented into sourcing, recruiting, and career paths. So, rather than shift to it on a role-by-role basis, I recommend making it a company-wide initiative to define if it is the right move for your business. It will involve creating a robust skills framework for all roles, learning to assess and interview candidates for skills rather than more personal and biased measures like culture fit, and designing onboarding and career paths that give employees the opportunity to upskill. Talent Marketplace technology providers that could assist include Gloat, 365 Talents, ProFinda, and Fuel50.

The Sell

In Career Builder's 2023 survey, a staggering 36% of managers admitted to lying to candidates about the role or company during the hiring process.[5] Of those, 75% lied during the interview, 52% in the job description, and 24% even lied in the offer letter. Managers admitted that they most commonly lie about the responsibilities, growth opportunities and career development opportunities, the company culture, benefits, commitment to social issues, the financial health of the company, and compensation.

The respondents also shared that 92% of misled candidates accepted the job, but 55% quit after being hired on false pretences: 14% in the first week, 35% in the first month, and 31% within three months. Failed recruitment is expensive and stressful, so it is imperative to be genuine. Truthfully selling the opportunity throughout the hiring process is also critical if you are not inundated with applicants; this starts with the job description, through all interviews, and includes during the offer negotiation. To assist, I crowdsourced some questions that can help you keep it realistic.

Australian Talent Acquisition Lead Mark Mansour likes to ask, especially of new managers:

- *What are your thoughts on who we are as a brand and what we do as a business?*
- *What is your understanding of the career path and internal mobility?*
- *How long do people stay? What's your attrition like?*
- *Where do people go when they leave you?*

Steve Levy suggests trying these questions:

- *Why would this person leave a competitor and come and work for you?*
- *What work are they doing at your company that they won't be doing at a competitor?*

Debi Easterday goes one further and always asks her managers this question:

- *If someone you loved was applying for a position with this company, what would you warn them about?*

Debi explained, 'When I talk to candidates about the role, I like to inform them of the good, the bad, and the ugly. If aspects of the culture will be deal-breakers regarding the long-term relationship, those "warts" will eventually reveal themselves. So, why not just point them out in advance?' I agree; be genuine if you don't want people leaving soon after you have invested time, money, and hassle into recruiting them.

People like vulnerability and authenticity. When I finish delivering a keynote, I can be asked a question that doesn't relate to my presentation or expertise, and I have gained immense respect by simply saying, 'I don't know. Can anyone in the audience answer?' Admitting that I cannot answer is better than blundering my way through it and looking foolish. Plus, there is power in openness and realism, which is too undervalued in the world of work, that people respect.

Hiring someone who knows all the "bad" stuff and is excited to join anyway makes business sense. The founders of Open Org say, 'Transparency is a driver for real, impactful change.' In their 'Case for Transparency', they share that besides it helping attract candidates who align with values, 70% of employees feel more engaged when senior leadership communicates openly, higher trust leads to a 76% increase in employee engagement and 29% better satisfaction, and highly engaged teams elevate performance and reap 21% greater profitability.[6]

Turning the Tables

It was inevitable that job seekers would start supporting themselves online; interview questions are visible on Glassdoor, in Reddit threads, and on community sites like Blind. However, Open Org has taken it one step further and published a list of some of the 'most spicy, authentic and hard-hitting questions' they could find that candidates can ask interviewers.[7] Below are seven of them to consider.

- *Why did the last three people leave your team?*
- *What was the last mistake the CEO admitted to?*
- *When has someone not succeeded here, and why?*
- *When were you last pushed to your limit? How did you get through it?*
- *Without using stats, how is the company doing with DEI?*
- *What's the business doing about the gender pay gap?*
- *What financials does the business share with you?*

Be sure to check the rest out at bit.ly/OO-questions (case sensitive) because they will help you genuinely sell the role, your leadership style, the culture, and the company. There may be several there you wouldn't want to answer, but it is better to consider them as you might be asked.

Call in Talent Acquisition

Now is the perfect time to bring in your talent acquisition partner. Even before approval, they can help you ensure that the profile you are creating is realistic – so you don't overpromise your boss or stakeholders – by adding their expertise and market knowledge. Of course, be honest and transparent that the role is awaiting approval! But if they know that it is in the pipeline, it means when they speak to applicants about other roles, they might identify someone suitable for this one when it does receive sign-off.

They can also help you take this shoddy first draft and make it into a standard job description for internal purposes and a job advertisement that will appeal to potential recruits. Though it could be tempting to use something like Chat GPT to assist here, the risk is that the output sounds like every other job advertisement or it becomes grandiose and lacking in authenticity.

Perfection is a myth; we are all perfectly imperfect. So, be open to having your assumptions and list of "must haves" challenged. Your talent acquisition partner should dissuade you from seeking an A-plus candidate for a B-minus role because the new hire won't stay if you overpromise and underdeliver. Ultimately, they can only save you time, money, and hassle if you work together and recruit against a realistic job description.

To satisfy your curiosity, ask your talent acquisition partner to conduct some searches to see the feasibility of your requirements. Mark Mansour challenges must-have requirements with, 'But do you really?' He told me,

Nobody needs a 10/10 new hire unless they are a startup with fewer than five employees! It is better to hire someone to train, which creates loyalty; treat them well, and they'll stay. By sitting with the manager and running searches, I can show them who is available and which companies we compete with. Job seekers can see a lot of information online, including reputation, remote or hybrid working and salary. We must be realistic and honest and not mess them around, or future hiring will be difficult!

As you peruse profiles, you may see some that interest you more than others, containing elements you haven't yet articulated. If the role is signed off, and it is more likely the person would reply to you, consider messaging or connecting with them. You may receive a better response, though that depends on your LinkedIn profile's quality, as I discuss in Chapter 7.

Compensation

As a forthright, assertive Australian, I have strong opinions about salary transparency and when the conversation around compensation should happen. I will never understand why companies waste time hiding it and even knock people out of the process for asking about it upfront. Everyone has bills to pay and a standard of living they would like to maintain or improve, so it's only natural to want to understand the compensation package early. And why waste time, money, and hassle interviewing someone who will never say yes?

Of course, if your company has not standardised compensation packages across employees and removed imbalances created by -isms, I can understand why salary transparency can be unsettling. Though I acknowledge that you work for a business seeking to generate profit and could even feel justified underpaying some of your current employees, pay discrepancies will come out because of the clarity created by the internet.

The demand for salary transparency is growing, especially around pay gaps. For example, on the 27 February 2024, the Australian Workplace Gender Equality Agency published the base salary and total remuneration median gender pay gaps for private sector employers with 100 or more employees.[8] The results show that 30% of Australian employers have a gender pay gap between the target range of plus or minus 5%, 8% less than –5% in favour of women, and 62% are over 5% in favour of men. Overall, 50% of all employers have a gender pay gap greater than 9.1%. It will be interesting to see how many resignations follow these results. I share tips for ensuring you don't worsen the gender pay gap in Chapter 5.

Gather data from candidates and sites like Salary.com to gauge if the salary is realistic. The big players in your field may offer far more than your company can, but if you know you cannot pay as well, there is little point hiding it. It is good that advertising the salary will stop some people from applying; people deselecting themselves saves you time interviewing someone you cannot afford to hire. Others will apply because they choose the work or your company's mission over the pay. You also have the option to grow the person you need through an internal promotion or hiring and training someone less experienced.

If you have a cap that makes salary negotiation challenging, consider what you could offer as an enticement. Other ways to compete include extra vacation, a sign-on bonus, flexibility on the start date, hybrid and remote work, self-development budgets, continued education, health and pension perks beyond statutory, and so on.

Jobs of the Future

Before I make suggestions for remote and alternative ways of working, which are most relevant for recruiting in highly competitive labour markets, here are some pertinent insights from the World Economic Forum's 'The Future of Jobs

Report'.[9] Respondents were from 803 companies employing over 11.3 million workers across 27 industry clusters and 45 economies worldwide, and the survey results were published on 30 April 2023.

- Technology-related roles, including AI and machine learning specialists, sustainability experts, business intelligence analysts, and information security analysts, or renewable energy-related roles, including renewable energy engineers, solar energy installation and system engineers, are the fastest growing.
- Education, agriculture, digital commerce and trade expect to see massive job growth.
- Analytical and creative thinking remain the most important skills for workers in 2023.
- 60% of workers require training before 2027, but only 50% can access adequate training opportunities now.
- An inability to attract talent and skill gaps are current barriers to transformation.
- 48% state improving talent progression and career pathways is a critical way to increase talent attraction, which is ahead of offering higher wages or reskilling and upskilling.

Whether you are inundated with applicants or work in the growing industries above, to save time, money, and hassle when hiring, a thorough recruitment alignment meeting and proper partnering with Talent Acquisition are critical. However, as I usually work in industries with a talent shortage, such as technology, engineering, healthcare, etc., what follows comes from experience helping companies fix their recruitment and attract people with in-demand skills.

When, Where, and How

Like 20 to 25% of the global population, I am a Highly Sensitive Person. It's a genetic trait found in over 100 species; HSPs have senses – sight, hearing, touch, taste, and smell – that function at a higher level than neurotypical people. For me, it means in an open-plan office, I can become overwhelmed by the sounds, smells, and lights. It is where I am least productive; the thought of commuting again fills me with dread.

After over 14 years of working for myself, I am happily unemployable, and that's because I work when, where, and how I want. I am typing this while sitting on a plane to Kosovo, which is not the most comfortable place to work, but I feel inspired, which is rare for me on a flight. Primarily, I work from my home office in solitude and silence, in flow. I choose my hours to work when I feel the most productive; it's about output and happy clients, not time at my desk. It's fair to say I am biased towards remote, flexible, and hybrid work, but I shall attempt to park my bias to encourage you to consider options objectively.

Presenteeism

> *Presenteeism is the act of staying at work longer than usual, or going to work when you are ill, to show that you work hard and are important to your employer.*[10]

My former managers will tell you I do the work well, while occasionally being awkward, and that I loathe presenteeism. At Spring Technology, my contracted hours were 9 am to

5.30 pm, but I started at 8.30 am each day to make the commute bearable. I also regularly worked through half of lunch and would stay back if a client required it. I hit or exceeded my target every month. Then a new director appeared and told us we must work until 6 pm – without increased pay. So, within my rights, I continued to leave at 5.30 pm daily. I achieved the set goals and departed at my contractual time because I had already given the company an extra hour each day. When I stayed back for client delivery reasons, I would see others were present but not working. They were just wasting their irreplaceable time each day to avoid being in trouble or taking advantage of situation bias to become the teacher's pet and get a promotion.

They were present; they were not productive.

However, presenteeism also happens when people complete work outside of office hours or on holiday. I distinctly remember the first time my professional boundary slipped due to mobile technology. It was 2006; I was on leave and utterly relaxed on a beach in southwest France. Foolishly, I answered a client call; she exploded in rage because somebody had walked away from the job offer and the person covering my work was "incompetent" – he most certainly was not! As an unhealed victim of childhood trauma, the outburst was taken straight to heart and remained a dark cloud over the rest of the break. Ultimately, the client's HR department created the failed hire, and, to this day, I wish I hadn't picked up the call.

Naïvely done, both Boomers and Generation X allowed mobile technology to negatively impact work-life balance. Now, with laptops and devices, work is seldom left at work at the end of the day; there is this perceived pressure to always be on. Unsurprisingly, burnout is rife.

Thankfully, though, companies can no longer ignore unhealthy presenteeism because millennials and Generation Z have watched our hustle culture and want it redefined with healthy boundaries. According to Deloitte's 2023 Gen Z and Millennial Survey of 22,000 Gen Z and millennials across 44 countries, 'While 49% of Gen Z and 62% of millennials say work is central to their identity, they place a strong focus on work/life balance — the top trait they admire in their peers and their top consideration when choosing an employer.'[11] Future employees will look for this in online reviews and threads.

Post-pandemic, high presenteeism isn't just about whether someone physically attends the office; it is also created by this "always on" culture, job and financial insecurity, and high workloads. The cost-of-living crisis is not helping those with inadequate sick leave, either. The cost to businesses from people being present – in the office or at home, or working while on leave or out-of-hours – when they are unwell or psychologically absent includes lost productivity, low morale, prolonged health issues, poor employee retention, and financial losses.[12]

The presenteeism I experienced was created by insecure leaders wanting to micromanage, which resulted in a toxic environment with low employee morale and productivity. If the internet had been as prevalent then as it is today, I would have left far sooner and written a scathing Glassdoor review to warn others. Today, people who know their worth will only tolerate an unhealthy work environment for so long, and they definitely won't want to join one.

Employees must be encouraged to switch off so that when they are present, they are productive, and unhealthy presenteeism doesn't deter future hires. In the aforementioned Deloitte survey, 82% of Gen Z and 80% of millennials also stated that mental health support and policies are important when considering an employer. So change is coming, but if the thought of relinquishing control and allowing your team to work where, when, and how they are most effective makes you shudder, it is time to get a leadership coach.

Of course, some jobs require people to be present, such as physical or manual tasks like providing human or animal healthcare, machinery and equipment operators, front-office retail, and hospitality, etc. However, as mentioned in Chapter 2, for those jobs that are achievable remotely or hybrid, your company has to decide if it wants to significantly reduce the available talent pool by mandating five days in the office for all roles.

According to another LinkedIn poll in February 2024, people seem undeterred by layoffs, with nearly 12,000 respondents: 56% want fully remote, 40% hybrid with 1 to 4 days at home, and just 3% want to be in the office five days each week.[13] Owl Labs' 2023 State of Hybrid Working survey found that if hybrid or remote employees were required to come to the office full-time, 41% wouldn't mind, 22% would go but be unhappy, 31% would start looking for other jobs, and 6% would quit.[14] That is 57% of people being less productive due to unhappiness or disengagement. Then there is gender bias; among the hybrid workers, 10% of women would quit compared to just 1% of men.

If candidates for this role work remotely or hybrid, and your company won't offer this, the hiring pool is diminished and will only get narrower in the years ahead.

Fake Flexibility and Exclusion

In a recent post, Sam Merron, a British Talent Acquisition Manager, said, 'I know the benefits of working in an office, so this isn't a naive take on this subject, but what does this stance mean for the wider demographic?'[15] He then shared the excluded people he knows:

The amazing person who is a wheelchair user and navigating through a major city is not impossible, but incredibly challenging, The amazing person who is Neurodiverse and struggles with too much interaction, noise and social cues. The amazing person who is a parent and having to juggle nursery/school times. The amazing person who is affected by the cost of living crisis and struggles to be able to pay for a train ticket. The amazing person who suffers from anxiety and the thought of being in a crowded train fills them with dread.

If you think of your friend network, can you add more to Sam's list? Without including working parents or those with disabilities, I can add several friends who suffer from chronic pain, one fighting cancer, two recovering from brain surgery, many enduring menopause and women-specific health issues, and even more caring for ageing and infirm parents. They are all capable employees; they simply need the flexibility that comes from remote or hybrid working. When they feel supported by their employers, they are happy, loyal and productive.

A survey by Careering into Motherhood of 2152 British working mums found that despite 92% of their employers being fully or partially receptive to flexible working requests, some managers expect full-time work to be completed within reduced hours or respond negatively to them.[16] Although legally entitled, 38% of working mothers had not asked for flexible work, with 46% believing that asking would impact future promotion opportunities. 40% of mothers also reported having had to complete work out of hours. Considering two-thirds of working mums also said that their level of ambition has increased or stayed the same, attitudes around this vital talent pool must change.

In March 2024, Lisa Taylor, a Talent Acquisition Lead, shared on LinkedIn:

> *My eldest daughter, who is now seven years old, was diagnosed with a brain tumour six years ago, becoming blind at diagnosis. I navigate chemotherapy and all of the other things that accompany being a parent of a child with additional needs, and I have a supportive husband (with a very supportive employer!) and family around to help. Yes, I am a carer, and I am a mother, but I absolutely can bring the best of me into work. I love working. It brings me a distraction from my situation and enables me to be 'me' outside of the oncology world.*[17]

Picture, through proper flexibility, making a great hire that also helps them keep their professional identity. Imagine how happy, productive, and easy they would be to retain, too.

Without overlooking fathers, Rich Lewis-Jones, Vice President of Asia Pacific at Smart Recruiters, posted on LinkedIn about his employer's flexibility and home-work; it is true employee advocacy:

> *I've been there to see my son sit up on his own for the first time, his first crawl, his first time holding his bottle, and so many more moments. I wouldn't have seen any of this if I was travelling to work, to sit behind a desk to please someone who only wanted me there because they didn't have the same flexibility options when they were in my position. If you are a CHRO or anyone on the C-Suite, I urge you to let your workforce (that can) work from home with complete flexibility. Your trust and enablement in them to be able to minimise missing magic moments*

that my employer has maximised for me, you will be paid back dividends in loyalty and performance across the board (when you hire the right people).[18]

In Chapter 5, I will expand on the cost of inflexible management and other -isms and phobias on hiring and share examples of how the internet reveals it to potential employees.

Job Share

With an ageing population who will have to work longer but may want to work fewer hours, and with a young generation who need to take on side hustles to make ends meet, this is just one example of how offering a job share could be a great way to attract and retain talent.

Job sharing is a flexible arrangement where two employees work part-time schedules sharing the same role. Benefits to your company include having double the expertise and a broader range of skills, knowledge, and creativity in the role, seamless holiday and sickness cover, increased motivation, better relationships with colleagues, and increased productivity.

In 'The benefits of job sharing – are two heads better than one?', lawyer Debra Gers says effective communication is vital.[19] 'When it works well, with two employees accountable to each other, working together, both not wanting to let the other one down, they may well be more productive and creative than one person carrying out that role.' She suggests getting clear on the basics and responsibilities for each person, judging their performance individually, setting pro-rata holidays and benefits, and, if looking for a job share partner, including the current employee in the hiring process.

Besides possible inexperience in managing a job share, is anything truly stopping you from offering it for this role? Just imagine the talent pool you could open up.

Part-Time

Can this role be fulfilled part-time? If possible, you will open up several pools of talent, including return-to-workers and people with side hustles who don't want to work full-time; the pandemic allowed many people to reassess their life choices. Critically, it could also be a way to retain your older workers and create space for the next generation.

Employment data from the OECD in 2022 revealed that people want part-time jobs; The Netherlands leads the way with 35% in part-time employment – defined as people whose primary employment (employee or self-employed) is usually fewer than 30 hours each week. Australia, Switzerland, and Japan sit at 25%, Germany, the UK, and Austria at around 22%, and Norway, Ireland, and New Zealand at around 20%.[20]

Research carried out by Bain & Company revealed that 150 million jobs will shift to older workers by 2030; Canada, Germany, the UK, Japan, the US, France, and Italy will all have 25% of the workforce over 55 by 2031.[21] 'Populations are ageing; work lives are lengthening. Fewer young people are entering the workforce due partly to lower fertility rates and partly to longer education.' Further in, they add, 'Yet it's rare to see organisations put programmes in place to integrate older workers into their talent system.' Considering 'the conventional moaning about a shortage of talent, skill gaps, and the weakening loyalties of younger workers to their firms', this seems an enormous oversight.

Here in the UK, for example, they raised the retirement age to 66, and rumour has it that they will look to push it higher. Not everyone has the stamina or health to work that long, but for those who can, it doesn't mean they want to retire, either. An analysis of ONS data in 2023 by Rest Less found a 56% increase in the over-50s working part-time since 2003; 66% of people working past 65 and 40% aged 60–64 worked part-time.[22] For part-time work to succeed, though, people must also dispel the misconception that it equates to lower-level work.

For all of your older employees, Bain & Company suggests a three-step approach to empowering them: 'Retain and recruit older workers by understanding what motivates them at work; reskill them for your next ten years of capability needs; and respect their strengths and allow them to do what they do best.' In Chapter 5, I discuss the cost of ageism, which also needs an attitude shift if companies are to retain or hire the expertise of senior workers.

Reboot Views

Be wary of holding onto views that reduce your potential hiring pool, which may not have even been yours to begin with. Unfounded beliefs like "great people aren't made redundant" have been proven to be nonsense during the 2020s rollercoaster. Layoffs have been akin to a lucky dip draw! Many people whose careers were stable, until March 2020 suddenly and without validation made them look like unreliable hires.

Gaps and Short Tenures

Stacey Bullock, a British Talent Manager, shared a LinkedIn post that started, "Yesterday, I spoke to somebody who had four jobs over five years. What a job hopper. . ." and she listed the reasons why she is anything but a job hopper:

Job 1: Started end of 2019 and she was let go when COVID hit. Job 2: A maternity cover with a set end date that she secured just one month later. Job 3: She accepted a role that was advertised as remote, but it turned into the need to travel to the office in London once a week; she lives in Liverpool. Job 4: After securing a role at a more local company, she was then let go in a wave of redundancies just five months later.[23]

Stacey ended with, 'This "job hopper" turned out to be one of the most resilient, dedicated and loyal candidates I have spoken to, and any company would be lucky to have her!'

Though I would like to believe that more people are like Stacey and that gap-ism or preconceived ideas about supposed "job hopping" have changed in the rollercoaster of recent years, this baseless bias can persist. Considering the ample evidence of job insecurity and how challenging securing new work has become, sticking to outdated views costs companies the chance to recruit capable and easy-to-retain people.

Presumptions about someone's work history, even the assumption that because someone is working they are a better applicant, can lead to mis-hires. As recruitment and leadership coach Angela Cripps recently noted, 'Just because they are good in one company doesn't mean they'll be just as good in another and vice versa.' So, instead of dismissing an applicant without evidence or explanation, look beyond the gaps and short tenures and assess the person's capability to perform the role's duties in the interview process.

Boomerang Hires

Who do you know who you could rehire or are you among the two-fifths of managers reluctant to hire a returning employee?[24] If it is the latter, let's consider the pros and cons of rehiring a former employee in terms of saved time, money, and hassle, just in case it is the right move for this role.

Pros	Cons
Less risk: there are performance records to peruse, for starters.	You must resolve former issues before they return; old ones might reignite.
Because you know them, you could hire them swiftly.	They might be resistant to any changes that have happened in their absence.
They will hit the ground running, needing little training and onboarding.	You could overlook a better candidate because this person is known.
They choose to return, so they should be more committed to staying.	Performance tends to remain the same and is surpassed by internal and external hires.
They return with fresh perspectives, knowledge, and skills.	They are more likely to turn over than both internal and external hires.

The last two cons are from a 2021 *Harvard Business Review* study that analysed a large dataset of eight years of archival data on over 30,000 employees who initially were external hires, promoted internal hires, or boomerang employees, placed into management positions at a large retail organisation.[25]

The report concludes, 'The bottom line is that boomerang employees are likely to be about the same as before, rather than better or worse, upon rehiring. First, consider your organisation's objectives, and if predictability, short-term performance, and lower training costs are your goals, boomerang employees may be right for you.' This study did not include layoff data, nor does it take into account the upheaval of the last four years, so be sure to factor that in when evaluating a potential boomerang hire.

Gaps, short tenures, and boomerangs are just some of the views I would like to see rebooted; in Chapter 5, I share many more that can cost companies dearly, both in terms of current and future hiring. As tempting as it might be to skip, for the sake of your company's Talent Acquisition, don't.

Chapter Summary

- Bad hires are expensive financially and on productivity and morale; you can avoid them by taking the time at the beginning of the process to consider who you need thoroughly.
- Create a rough draft by answering the questions, enriching them with more answers from your team; honesty matters to successful recruitment and retention.
- Ask Talent Acquisition to help you make the profile realistic and create a formal job description and an appealing job advertisement.
- To increase the talent pool, consider implementing healthy flexible or hybrid working, job sharing, part-time, or boomerang hires.
- Watch for bias from old-fashioned views of candidates' gaps and short tenures that aren't realistic in the 2020s.

5

The Cost of -Isms and Phobias on Hiring

Does your latest job advertisement or website's career page say something like, 'We are committed to Equal Opportunities and welcome applications from all sections of the community'? Is that a true reflection of your company's hiring process?

Founder of the charity Radical Recruit Emma Freivogel raised this while asking people to look around their office to identify a representative from all sections of the community. She challenges the intent of this statement.[1] Does it mean single parents, ex-offenders, people without degree education, domestic violence survivors, disabled people, people of colour, transgender people, victims of modern-day slavery, over fifties, fat people, people with experience of the care system or young people? She witnesses the cost of -isms daily as someone committed to helping those furthest away from the labour market to become recruitment-ready, and she has earned the right to call out managers and leaders when she sees hypocrisy.

She is not alone. Today, countless people share on social media and review sites their experiences of discrimination, which is when one person or group of people is treated less fairly or less well than other people or groups, or bias, which is the tendency to prefer one person or thing to another and to favour that person or thing.[2, 3] These online insights into the experiences of an employee or candidate can make future hiring difficult.

-isms and phobias are discriminatory and often hostile beliefs and behaviours based on stereotypes, fear, and ignorance.[4] There are more than I could ever fit into one chapter, so I aim to show the impact of some of them and leave you with the awareness that any -ism or phobia can lead to online posts and reviews that negatively impact recruitment and retention.

Though I accept that we are all perfectly imperfect humans doing the best we can each day, if these are left unchecked and unchallenged, the cost to hiring will be high, and worse for the recipient, who may have become the best person you ever recruited.

In this chapter, I have focused on sharing recruitment examples and have recommended further reading from bias experts in each section. I hope you will consider your company and behaviour through a new lens and fix any lingering -isms or phobias because one thing is sure: the internet isn't going anywhere anytime soon!

Sexism

The belief that the members of one sex are less intelligent, able, skilful, etc., than the members of the other sex, especially that women are less able than men. Also, the treatment of men and women based on the belief that particular jobs and activities are suitable only for men and others are suitable only for women.[5]

My feed in the last 24 hours alone has highlighted the ingrained issue of sexism. First, I saw an agenda for a two-day AI & The Future of Work virtual event, with a line-up containing 30 male and just five female speakers. Then I read about the Oscars snubbing female director Greta Gerwig and actress Margot Robbie, who together created the biggest blockbuster of 2023 and the highest-grossing movie ever directed by a woman. Let's also not forget the behaviour of the male host of the Golden Globes towards

Taylor Swift, who had the highest-grossing music tour ever, surpassing $1 billion in revenue, and his anti-feminist comments about the *Barbie* movie, which unintentionally highlighted the sexism the film addresses.

It makes me wonder what women need to do to prove their professional worth, but let me bring it closer to home. Have you ever asked your female circle, say, your mother, sister, aunt, cousin, or friends, about their experiences of sexism in the workplace? If you identify as female or non-binary, you probably have. If you identify as male, you may be horrified by what you hear. Ask them about their experiences. Though I hope that the patriarchy will one day fall, sadly, misogyny is alive and well in workplaces in 2024.

Writing this as a company founder, UK resident, and white Australian female who has the freedom to express herself and travel freely, I acknowledge my privilege and the lens through which I experience life and now speak about sexism and its impact on hiring. Sadly, around the world, not everyone who identifies as female has these same fundamental freedoms.

In 1959, when my mother became engaged to her first husband, she was forced to resign from her position in the bank. Engaged, not even married and certainly not pregnant. I don't know where you reside as you read this, but in the UK in 2024, this sounds preposterous and would never happen. But over the last 15 years, I have witnessed an exceptional female director be managed out of a company while pregnant. I have also seen women recruited while pregnant, something that wouldn't have happened a few decades ago.

Discussing this topic with a client, they shared that recently, a manager – in a company priding itself on inclusivity – told an interviewee outright that he wouldn't hire her because she was pregnant. The candidate declared this during the application and was informed it wasn't an issue, but the manager ignored Talent Acquisition's notes. Such a blatant statement left this company open to legal repercussions. Thankfully, the recruiter stepped in and found the interviewee a job in another team. Whew!

Though it may seem that the West has come a long way in a short period of time, everyday sexism is so ingrained into society that it takes conscious effort to stop it. You will be called out for it publicly if you don't, though.

Mansplaining

Mansplaining happens when a man, often inaccurately and usually while interrupting, explains something to a woman in a condescending tone. As a perfect example, you may have seen the viral video of professional golfer Georgia Ball's practice session. Feeling superior with his 20 years of experience, a man interrupted her repeatedly and told her what was wrong with what she was doing. He continued his unsolicited advice each time she tried to speak up to explain that she was working on a swing change.[6]

Somehow, Georgia kept her cool, but a recent *Fortune* article stated that mansplaining could make women question their workplace competence and self-worth, and it can even stunt their careers.[7] Women will also avoid working with those who mansplain, making team collaboration less productive and costly.

But it doesn't just happen to employees; in under a minute, I found countless Glassdoor Interview reviews citing mansplaining. One for ETX Capital says, 'Interviewing with their ninja/rockstar team lead was a very strange experience. They spent the first 15 minutes mansplaining basic aspects of the .Net frameworks and currency trading to me.

(I have over 30 years of experience, including over 20 years in .Net. And I trade currencies in my spare time.) It was as if they hadn't read my CV.'[8] This one is for IPI Singapore, 'The ultimatum for me was when they took 15 minutes of the session mansplaining the definition of "Advisory." It felt berating. Honestly, I did not get a good sense of whether they knew what they were truly looking for in the first place.'[9] Not knowing who they are looking for also indicates that they don't understand the importance of the recruitment alignment meeting.

Queen Bee Syndrome

Research from The Workplace Bullying Institute found that women are bullied by other women up to 65% of the time.[10] It is called Queen Bee Syndrome, and it happens when senior women purposefully hold back other women because of their gender.[11] With the patriarchy alive and well, and only 8.8% female Fortune 500 CEOs and fewer female leadership roles available, the more senior women get, sadly, it's unsurprising that some women – consciously or unconsciously – undermine other women to get ahead.[12] It was also easy to find an example of a woman being sexist to another during recruitment.

On LinkedIn, Georgina Hughes posted about her interview:[13]

The interviewer explained the pressure the coaches in her organisation faced and asked if I could manage a high-pressure job while being a mum. She told me she was not a parent and that her sister, who has children, didn't have time to talk to her. She said, "Woman to woman, how do you feel about this?" When I told her I had worked in high-pressure environments, she said, "Yeah, but that was before you had kids." Not only is this sexist and so not cool, it's illegal.

Besides being a question a father would not be asked, Georgina is correct; in many countries, it is illegal, so be sure to include all employees when you look to address any sexist workplace behaviour.

Gender Pay Gap

Fixing any gender or other -ism-related pay gap is wise because people talk with their colleagues, impacting productivity, and online, affecting hiring.

On March 8th each year, the well-loved bias-outing tool, Gender Pay Gap Bot, can be seen in action @PayGapApp on the site formerly known as Twitter.[14] Using publicly available government data, it retweets posts made by companies on International Women's Day, adding the percentage of the gender pay gap. It's not biased: it will also show when men receive less pay. But the genius is in the retweet; if a company's social media team tries to hide the evidence by deleting the original post, the retweet will still show the company name and pay gap percentage. The tweets average around 15,000 views each, increasing exponentially each March.

Public humiliation aside, when companies with diverse teams are 33% more likely to outperform on profitability, and 76% of job seekers look for a diverse workforce, it makes business sense to fix pay gaps.[15, 16] To get an idea of where your company is now, look at Equidi, a world-first platform that shows you the real-time pay gap and workforce representation across every part of your business on a single dashboard. It will take all of the frustration out of fixing the issue.

Stop Asking for Their Current Salary Appallingly, in a quick search to find an example of how the pay gap is exacerbated and perceived by interviewees, I found another woman-undermining-woman example. The post on Reddit says:

> *I just had an interview in which the recruiter asked for my salary expectations; I turned the question back and asked what the salary range was. She responded, "I've been doing this for 27 years; it doesn't make sense to disclose the salary if it's 30k more or less than you're already making." I can't believe she said it doesn't make sense for someone to increase their salary by that much. I finally just pitched the range that was common for the position, according to Google. I think it's BS that companies only want to pay you 5k more than your last job; this contributes to the pay gap.*[17]

Testing this recruiter's theory. A man and a woman apply for a role and have the same skills, everything equally. But she's on 40k, whilst he's on 55k, and the role has been budgeted for and signed off at 60k. According to this recruiter's biased thinking, the female applicant only deserves to increase her salary to 45k, while the male applicant can receive the whole 60k. Whereas by not asking about the applicant's current salary, and just stating that the salary is 60k, whoever gets the job gets 60k. If the female applicant gets it, the gender pay gap closes, and she is paid fairly for her skills and experience. Importantly, if she later compares her salary to her peers, she won't feel resentment, impacting productivity, or leave, creating the expense of failed recruitment and rehiring.

This post also reinforces that all employees, and any external recruiters you partner with, need to be educated about sexism and the problem with asking for current salary.

State the Salary Gen Z will make up 30% of the workforce by 2030, and according to Adobe's Future Workforce Study, 85% of upcoming and recent grads are less likely to apply if the company does not disclose the salary range on the job advertisement.[18] Before you roll your eyes, thinking, 'Back in my day,' 38% of respondents on my LinkedIn poll said they would not apply to a job that didn't state the salary. Scanning the faces of those who said no, their ages appear to range from 25 to 65. Another 17% said 'it depends' and added comments indicating they would be looking for the fastest way to find the salary so they didn't waste everyone's time.[19] Losing 38% of applicants and a potential 17% more seems crazy when there is such an easy alternative.

The issue of salary transparency will only worsen as future generations enter the workforce. It is time to state the salary on the job advertisement and pay the successful applicant based on how you value what they bring to the role and the company. Let's stop paying people based on how their current employer values or, possibly, does not value them. Sites like Salary.com, Salary Expert, Payscale, Salary Explorer, or Glassdoor expose market salaries, so paying someone below market rate can create a costly retention problem. Lowballing leads to resentment and failed recruitment or employment, and this churn can also impact the productivity of your current employees.

Speaking of productivity, a Bocconi University Business Research paper, using the pay transparency data of US academics, found that if a company had been equitable and consistent in its allocation of pay against performance, then the overall employee response on productivity was positive.[20] But they found the opposite was also true! So, though the thought of salary transparency and increases could have leaders shaking in their boots, it seems inevitable. As it impacts productivity, it seems wise to get ahead of it.

In the US, it has already become law in many states to advertise the role's salary, but without considering the negative impact on the employer brand, job postings are appearing with ridiculous ranges like $0 to $250,000. On the other extreme, my British friend is a resident of the UAE and shared that the salary is only disclosed in the offer letter, where it is usually found to be far too low and, of course, rejected. Not only is this a waste of everyone's irreplaceable time and worsening the pay gap, but it is also costly to start the hiring process again and could mean delays to projects and even lost clients.

Return-to-Workers Deserve Fair Pay A 2023 British study by the Trade Unions Congress found that one in 5 men cannot afford to take paternity leave at all due to the low level of statutory paternity pay, and 53% of families struggle financially when dads or partners take paternity leave.[21] The gender pay gap doesn't help; it forces women into the primary caring role because of finances. However, the sexist attitude is also ingrained into society and the workplace, evidenced by a CIPD survey that found that three-quarters of men felt there was a stigma attached to taking paternity leave, with nearly all respondents agreeing that the workplace culture needed to change.[22] Another survey conducted by Ipsos Mori also found that 45% of both parents and non-parents agreed that taking time off work to care for a child harms a person's job.[23]

Senior Manager Rebecca Collis shared her experience returning to work:

I left as a civil servant, which meant that I had great benefits but a pretty poor salary, and, to be honest, I had been undervaluing myself for years. It took a genuinely consultative recruiter to tell me that the skills that I had acquired were worth so much more. I am truly thankful because, without his advice, I would have taken another lesser job that would not have suited my abilities and where my strategic approach would have been out of place and even caused irritation.

By helping Rebecca realise her worth, she was happy and productive in the role and wasn't a source of annoyance for colleagues.

On parental leave, people gain skills that include time management, planning, multi-tasking, crisis management, delegation, communication, and negotiation. Life as a new parent also means they need to learn skills quickly, and when they return from leave, they bring these back into the workplace. So, if you are hiring a return-to-worker, don't widen the gender pay gap by thinking they don't deserve the same remuneration as someone currently employed. Instead, consider that they have gained valuable skills while away from the workplace, which will swiftly counter any skills that may have become a little rusty.

Judging Appearance and Attire

Asking my female friends about their experiences of being judged for their appearance and attire led to 97 speedy responses. Financial Services VP Suzanne Wolko shared that she was once told by a senior executive that her boss wouldn't hire her if she kept her manicure. She said, 'He prefers no polish on women.'

Lisa Baldock MBE added that she once didn't get a job in a library because she was wearing her hearing aids. She was asked if she could cover them with her hair while working, which seems ironic and is definitely ableist. These days, similar behaviour is prohibited in many countries. In 2023, a federal jury awarded $1,675,000 to a deaf applicant who was passed over for two warehouse positions by McLane Northeast because, under the Americans with Disabilities Act, companies are prohibited from discriminating against qualified applicants based on their disability.[24]

Researching online, it didn't take long to find recent sexist interviewers.

On Feelberry Global Consulting's website, under jobs, the Finnish company boldly states 'fairness with inclusivity' in capital letters, starkly contrasting with four of the last six Glassdoor Interview reviews from people judged on their appearance.[25] One review says, 'The guy interviewing me only cared about looks and even body-shamed me. He didn't care about my qualifications or previous experience, just that I didn't have the correct look for the job. He even said that because I am chubby, people might not take me seriously.'[26] Saying you have fairness with inclusivity is not enough; you must demonstrate it. Most people loathe hypocrisy and will shout about it.

Imagine being mocked by an interviewer for the content of your Master's thesis and then hearing, 'He proceeded to advise me that I was wasting my time looking for work in Tokyo, "looking the way you look."' This humiliation was inflicted on an interviewee by the COO of Slate Consulting and shared in a Glassdoor Interview review as a warning to others.[27] Five potential recruits have found the review helpful so far; five people who won't have applied.

Further Reading

- Book: *Don't Fix Women: The Practical Path to Gender Equality At Work* by Joy Burnford.
- Book: *Flexible Working: How to Implement Flexibility in the Workplace to Improve Employee and Business Performance* by Gemma Dale.
- Blogs: Textio or Ongig – software companies eliminating bias in job advertisements.

Transphobia and Cissexism

> *Transphobia is the harmful or unfair things a person does based on a fear or dislike of transgender and non-binary* people. Policies, behaviours, rules, etc., that result in a continued unfair advantage to cisgender† people and unfair or harmful treatment of transgender and non-binary people.*[28]
>
> *Cissexism refers to prejudice or discrimination on the basis of sex, especially towards transgender or gender-expansive‡ people. Includes the assumption that being cisgender is more natural or superior.*[29]
>
> * Non-binary: people whose gender does not match the body they were born with.
> † Cisgender: people whose gender matches the body they were born with.
> ‡ Gender Expansive: people who may be cisgender, identify with a mix of genders or not identify with a gender at all.

In a 2023 global survey across 30 countries, 3% of respondents identify as transgender, gender fluid, non-binary, or other.[30] Research from McKinsey found in the US:[31]

- Transgender adults are twice as likely to be unemployed, and those who are employed earn 32% less than their cisgender colleagues, even with comparable or greater skills and education.
- Over half of transgender employees are uncomfortable being out at work and feel far less supported in the workplace and by managers. They also find it harder to get promoted.

- A concerted effort to increase inclusion, employment, and wage equity for transgender people could boost annual consumer spending in the US by $12 billion per annum.

No matter your personal beliefs, it is statistically likely that you already have employees who don't identify as cisgender and are hiding their identity, which is impacting their mental health and productivity.

Plus, a poll from Gallup found that:

The proportion of U.S. adults who consider themselves to be lesbian, gay, bisexual or transgender has grown at a faster pace over the past year than in prior years. This is occurring as more of Generation Z is reaching adulthood. These young adults are coming of age, including coming to terms with their sexuality or gender identity, at a time when Americans increasingly accept gays, lesbians and transgender people, and LGBT individuals enjoy increasing legal protection against discrimination.[32]

The research also says that they expect the proportion of LGBT Americans to exceed 10% soon. Just imagine the negative impact of those employees, if not made to feel welcome, included, and supported at work, on morale and productivity, and the cost of churn as they leave for employment with better leaders.

Pronouns and Misgendering

In countries where it is legal for someone to openly identify as LGBTQIA+, one of the easiest ways to spot transphobia relates to a person's acceptance or use of pronouns. My pronouns, for example, are She/Her, and I will explain more about them in Chapter 7.

When I received a review for my book, *The Robot-Proof Recruiter*, that said, 'Very PC view of recruitment. I sent the book back after the advice was to announce to a client or candidate over the phone what your pronouns are,' I wasn't upset because I saw his prejudice. He put his real name on the review, which reveals that he is a recruiter in the construction industry. Would you want this biased recruiter working on your roles? I sure wouldn't!

Misgendering is when you use pronouns or a title that does not align with the person's gender identity. It can occur because someone assumes another's gender, says it by accident, or does it intentionally to create harm. Also, if asking for preferred pronouns and gender at the application, ensure that your applicant tracking system includes options to identify as non-binary or prefer-not-to-say.

I have a lovely trans client to whom I apologise when I mistakenly use she not they and I consciously try harder. They don't expect me to make a big deal of my mistake; I just acknowledge and correct it. They also warned me about the harm of deadnaming, which is when people intentionally use the trans person's birth name, which they no longer use since transitioning.

In the Reddit Trans community, I found a post titled, 'Turned down a job because I got misgendered in the interview, feeling bad about it.'[33] They went on to explain:

> *I get that misgendering happens. What really got me was that I was being interviewed by two people, and when one of them would misgender me, the other would visibly wince as they could tell it was happening but never said anything. I've had really bad experiences before working with transphobic supervisors and find getting misgendered every day to really impact my mental health. I recently worked at an LGBTQ place where it never happened, so I know I don't have to feel this way.*

If the thought of negatively impacting the mental health of an employee isn't motivation enough, the cost of restarting the hiring process and the impact on morale and productivity should be.

In another thread, I found this query:

I got laid off recently, and in an effort to get back to work ASAP, have been applying to places with my deadname (so prospective employers can verify references, so I avoid interview discrimination since I don't pass well, etc.) and I finally got an offer. I accepted it today. I'm filling out my paperwork, and the first thing I have to do is select my title (Mr, Ms, etc.) and male/female gender checkbox. I REALLY don't want to have to fill this out with my AGAB and deadname, but I don't know what to do.[34]

You could avoid placing applicants in this predicament by emulating a company like ThoughtWorks, which clearly shows its genuine inclusion on its Insight blog.

In a recent article, ThoughtWorks shared the Eleven Steps We Took for Trans Inclusion, which include using pronouns, educating, being an ally, supportive behaviours, publicly supporting the community, and more genuinely affirming actions.[35] With social media users quick to denigrate a company's hypocrisy, I hope you will read the article in full. However, there are two points worth highlighting, 'We simplified the process around name changes, and actively work to ensure these are handled in all our systems and with any third parties', and 'Policies are inclusive and gender neutral.' By publicly stating this, any LGBTQIA+ interviewee knows they can be open with a prospective employer and only need to worry about performing well at the interview.

Further Reading

- Book: *The New Gender Paradox: Fragmentation and Persistence of the Binary* by Judith Lorber.
- Book: *Real Gender: A Cis Defence of Trans Realities* by Danièle Moyal-Sharrock and Constantine Sandis.
- Website: Identiversity.

Heterosexism

> *Heterosexism is discrimination or prejudice against nonheterosexual people based on the belief that heterosexuality is the only normal and natural expression of sexuality.*[36]

Inclusive and fair employers see positive business outcomes, including higher productivity from LGBT workers, lower costs from absenteeism, and a lower likelihood of turnover.[37] According to another report from Research and Markets of 120 companies, diverse companies earn 2.5 times higher cash flow per employee, and inclusive teams are more productive by over 35%.[38] It is little wonder that many companies champion diversity, equity, inclusion and belonging, but it must ring true.

On Startek's website, it says, 'We believe diverse teams create better outcomes', and notes that they were recognised as one of the Best Companies for Diversity in 2022 by review site Comparably.[39] Yet on Comparably's competitor site, Glassdoor, an interviewee shared that she was asked by a Startek interviewer, 'Do you think you can perform this job well if you're not stable with your gender?' Her review of the interview says, 'The initial interview is all fine. But, I am very disappointed with the final interview question.

One questioning capabilities just because of being a lesbian. Too homophobic. Too unprofessional. And definitely not an INCLUSIVE organisation.'[40] To make things worse, this applicant was referred by an employee who will be feeling mortified.

If your company makes similar bold statements, all managers, leaders, and interviewers must be aware of the consequences of their actions not matching these policies. In this case, a lousy review to warn other job seekers and a disgruntled employee who will be unlikely to refer more people, which is a shame when employee referrals are considered the highest quality source of hire.

Further Reading

- Book: *The Economic Case for LGBT Equality: Why Fair and Equal Treatment Benefits Us All* by MV Lee Badget.
- Book: *Data-Driven DEI: The Tools and Metrics You Need to Measure, Analyze, and Improve Diversity, Equity, and Inclusion* by Randall Pinkett.
- Book: *Unf*cking Work* by Neil Usher with Kirsten Buck and Perry Timms.

Racism

Racism is the belief that people of some races are inferior to others, and the behaviour which is the result of this belief. Racism also refers to the aspects of a society which prevent people of some racial groups from having the same privileges and opportunities as people from other races.[41]

In my experience, travelling to 57 countries on six continents, living in Sydney, Australia, and London, UK, and working with clients worldwide, I have witnessed many forms of racism. Some expected. Some surprising. None justified. All disappointing.

Back trawling Reddit, I was soon directed to a LinkedIn job advertisement by Kate's Ice Cream in Portland, USA, for a Marketing Assistant.[42] It stated, 'We are prioritising hiring a woman or POC.' In contrast, further down, they said, 'Kate's Ice Cream does not and shall not discriminate on the basis of race, colour, religion (creed), gender, gender expression, age, national origin (ancestry), disability, marital status, sexual orientation, or military status, in any of its activities or operations. These activities include, but are not limited to, hiring and firing of staff, selection of volunteers and vendors, and provision of services.' It is clear what they are trying to achieve, but you cannot say no to white men or non-binary people while claiming that you do not discriminate on the basis of colour or gender and gender expression.

On the community site Blind, a user publicly shared:

> *I interviewed with SmartThings mobile team. The manager of Mountain View Mobile is racist. During the interview, he pulled his eyes with his hands and said Samsung engineers in Suwon are not good engineers. This is the worst interview experience I have had because I am Asian and was very offended by this man. This happened a few months ago, but I am still so mad!*[43]

The first reply was from an Engineer at SmartThings, 'Please DM me. I am at this company and suspect I know who you are talking about. That is completely inappropriate.' Not even a denial. The comments turned into a stream of incompatible viewpoints, but the company's reputation is damaged. The numerous negative interview reviews on other sites don't help either. SmartThings will find it challenging to hire engineers in the future.

Blind has its share of trolls, like all sites, but when enough people make similar comments, you know that the company has a problem, like the workforce management platform Rippling. A current employee posted:

> *I made the grave mistake of joining Rippling. I came from a FAANG company, and I'm on H1B. My boss figured out quickly that I am on a visa and is constantly threatening my job. "We need this faster. A citizen could do this faster. 60 days isn't that long to find a job in this market." I'm having panic attacks from the stress.*[44]

The post racked up 112 comments in 24 hours, with most people suggesting he record the conversations, approach his manager's manager (skip), take it to HR, take legal action, and even share the recordings on social media.

It may be illegal to share these recordings, but victims can get to the point where they don't care about the repercussions. Consider the further damage to Rippling's reputation if this happens. The employee is being bullied; his mobile device makes it easy to gather evidence, make his case, and permanently tarnish the company's reputation. With another 1,295 posts on Blind discussing the company and current employees advising interviewees to walk away, Rippling must fix its toxic culture!

Further Reading

- Book: *The Anti-Racist Organization: Dismantling Systemic Racism in the Workplace* by Shereen Daniels.
- Book: *Skin in the Game: Hidden Asymmetries in Daily Life* by Nassem Nicholas Taleb.
- Book: *UNBIAS: Addressing Unconscious Bias at Work* by Stacey A. Gordon.

Ageism

> *Ageism is the unfair treatment of people because of their age.*[45]

Jeff Shapiro, an American Talent Acquisition Director, has been running the job search gauntlet for a few months and sharing his experiences on LinkedIn. One post starts, 'Hello Ageism. Is That You?' (If you connect the tune, this will likely resonate more!) and he included a screenshot of a compulsory application question that introduces ageism, 'What year did you graduate from college?'[46] It also immediately discounts the people with a wealth of experience without tertiary education, which, in this instance, is not required for role success.

Late-Career Ageism

Ageism affects people of all ages, but I want to discuss late-career ageism. According to an article on Indeed, there are five career stages: Exploration 21–25, Establishment 25–35, Mid-Career 35–45, Late Career 45–55, and Decline 55–65.[47] I was rattled to discover that I am only a few years away from the bracket the writers consider a 'decline'! My work life is just getting interesting; how can it be in decline? My similarly-aged friend network was equally outraged by the term; they are thriving with no plans to decline into retirement. Which matters when we live longer and have fewer children in the West.

However, a mysterious thing happens as we age: we become invisible. Perhaps you are an older reader and have felt that moment when twenty and thirty-somethings no longer seem to notice your presence. In my forties and early fifties, I have found such happiness because I finally worked out who I am and became comfortable in my skin. I have the joy of experience and wisdom that comes with age while still feeling young. But not all in my age group feel that way, especially not if they are experiencing ageism while interviewing.

A survey of 83,000 people in 57 countries found that one in two respondents held high or moderate ageist stereo-types and prejudices.[48] Another study by the advocacy group AARP found that bias against 50-plus workers reduced GDP in the United States by around $850 billion in 2018, and they expect it to amount to $3.9 trillion by 2050.[49]

Ageism against those over 45 is a paradox, too. A study by Generation found that hiring managers, in different sectors across seven countries, consistently said they perceived that only 15–18% of the 45-plus-year-old interviewees were a fit for their roles.[50] But, when asked about the performance of those they hired in that age group, they stated that 87% of those individuals were performing as well, if not better, than their younger peers. They also said that 90% are viewed as having long retention potential, if not more so, than their younger peers. So what is this really about?

Leadership Coach and author of *Fire Well*, Sue Ingram, thinks it is about insecurity and explains, 'An insecure manager may not want to hire someone older as they might know more and judge them accordingly or possibly show them up to their peers. Whereas a secure manager would hire an older person and seek out and utilise all of their experience and hard-won expertise.'

This insecurity-based ageism is what I witnessed the most in 2023 among my network of talent acquisition professionals. This behaviour is a loss for those organisations, and it is concerning that the people responsible for attracting recruits are displaying this bias. With today's modern, less physically taxing jobs and evidence that senior hires can outperform their younger colleagues, is there a talent shortage, or is ageism at play?

Experience-ism

Reading an article in the *Employment Law Review* titled, '74% of job hunters are rejected entry level jobs due to lack of experience', I remembered trying to get a waitressing job in the early 1990s and being consistently knocked back for lack of experience.[51] I figured it couldn't be that hard to learn but was caught in a Catch-22. It makes me wonder at the short-sightedness of companies asking for experience for "entry-level" positions.

Engineering and Manufacturing Recruiter Mark Hopkins shared that over the years, his clients consistently demanded recruits be able to hit the ground running, i.e. be experienced. They think time is money, so they haven't invested time in training graduates, and this shortsightedness has left companies suffering from an ageing workforce. Mark said, "In 2022, 80% of my placements replaced retiring engineers. Companies were also shocked to discover that they now teach skills differently and have had to split roles into two or even three jobs. Thankfully, some are taking on graduates now, but I have others who have been trying to hire for over two years!" I suggested that Mark approach all of his recently retired engineers to see if any would consider returning on a part-time basis or a job share. It's worth a try, especially with those companies who refuse to face the reality of the skill shortage.

Further Reading

- Book: *Revolting Women: Why Midlife Women Are Walking Out, And What to Do About It* by Lucy Ryan.
- Book: *The Remix: How to Lead and Succeed in the Multigenerational Workplace* by Lyndsey Pollak.
- Book: *Wisdom at Work: The Making of a Modern Elder* by Chip Conley.

Ableism and Stigma

Ableism is discrimination or prejudice against individuals with disabilities.[52] Stigma is a set of negative and unfair beliefs that a society or group of people have about something.[53]

Someone with a disability has a physical, mental, cognitive, or developmental condition that impairs, interferes with, or limits a person's ability to engage in certain tasks or actions or participate in typical daily activities and interactions.[54] One in 6 people experience significant disability, and just 2% of those with disabilities use a wheelchair.[55] A staggering 80% have invisible disabilities, which include hearing or visual impairments, bipolar disorders, Alzheimer's disease, people with heart conditions, people with PTSD, chronic pain, and many more.[56]

Neurodivergence is a term used to describe differences in brain function; while in some cases, neurodivergent people may be protected by disability legislation, they might not automatically identify as disabled, and it is certainly not the same as mental illness. Classical definitions of neurodivergence include diagnoses of autism, ADHD, and dyslexia. Both neurodivergent and neurotypical people are part of neurodiversity. Stigma especially happens when people consider neurotypical people as 'normal' and neurodivergent people as 'abnormal'.

With today's technology and ease of remote work for many roles, there are few reasons to allow ableist hiring to continue. Plus, in the UK, the collective spending power of individuals with disabilities and their families and friends is called The Purple Pound.[57] In 2021, it was estimated at £274 billion per annum and over £16 trillion globally. When disabled individuals don't see themselves represented in a company's advertising or marketing, they can be less inclined to engage with the brand. It makes commercial sense to ensure you hire a diverse workforce and lose any ableism or stigmas, conscious or unconscious.

Falling at the First Hurdle   On Recruiting Hell again, after reading about the angst created by personality tests on neurodivergent applicants, I spied this thread. 'Why does "Please let us know about any disabilities so we can make reasonable adjustments" feel very much like "Please let us know about any disabilities so we can filter you out before we've even looked at your CV"?'[58] It is a dilemma! Tell the truth, and they could face rejection from companies that fear change or are reluctant to adapt.

Among the debate on the post, I shuddered reading this comment, 'I wear hearing aids in both ears and don't class myself as disabled, but I've had recruiters before straight up ask me why I've put not disabled when I'm wearing hearing aids. Are they even allowed to ask me this?'. You will need to refer to your country's relevant laws to know if asking this is permitted, but logic would dictate that this line of questioning will only make someone uncomfortable.

Thankfully, the original poster found some humour, 'What I really want to write is "I'm disabled enough to meet your diversity quotas but not disabled enough to cause any problems." Which is what they want anyway.' It is hard to argue against it, but if you want to be inclusive and open the door to more applicants, your company must find a way to show it is safe for people to be honest – which most in the thread suggested people not be! – and that it isn't a tick box exercise that falters people before they even apply.

Ban The Box

Speaking of falling at the first hurdle and stigmas, at the beginning of this chapter, Emma Freivogel mentioned ex-offenders. Including the check box that asks, 'Have you ever had a criminal conviction?' excludes a significant proportion of the population from applying.

Some stats that may surprise you: according to charity Unlock, here in the UK, for example, over 12 million people have a criminal record.[59] Nearly 70% of all sentences are fines, including driving offences. Fewer than 10% of those convicted go to prison. Yet, 27% of employers state they won't hire someone with a criminal record, which makes no sense if, for example, the conviction is a driving offence and driving isn't in the role's duties.[60]

The easy fix is to join a campaign like Ban The Box, remove the box and not ask about unspent criminal convictions on application forms. Timpson Group Companies says around 10% of their workforce is people with criminal convictions. They state, 'The vast majority of ex-offenders we recruit are extremely loyal, productive, hardworking and make excellent colleagues. Many have been promoted and fully grasped the second chance they have been given. To put it simply, recruiting ex-offenders has been great for our business.'[61]

Greyston Bakeries offers employment to anyone seeking a job and does so without the use of resumes, background checks, or interviews. They have a lot of advice for other employers on their website, including,

If employers openly state that they're hiring formerly incarcerated individuals and why, employees, customers, and vendors are able to make informed decisions about working alongside/with their new colleagues and share in the responsibility of maintaining healthy working relationships. Business success begins with loyal employees who work hard. Period. Employers simply miss out when they focus on someone's past; it's not where someone has been that matters; it's where they are going that counts.[62]

Further Reading

- Book: *A Dozen Brilliant Reasons to Employ Disabled People: Why Successful Businesses See Inclusion as an Asset Rather Than a Problem* by Jane Hatton.
- Website and training: Evenbreak: job board for disabled candidates.

- Book: *Neurodiversity at Work: Drive Innovation, Performance and Productivity with a Neurodiverse Workforce* by Theo Smith and Amanda Kirby.
- Website: Greyston Bakeries – Open Hiring.

Final Few

Despite all the -isms mentioned in this chapter, as well as the gap-ism, presenteeism, and classism noted in Chapter 4, unfortunately, there are still more -isms and phobias excluding people from employment.

In June 2023, the VP of the European Commission, Margaritis Schinas, said, 'Far too many refugees could not find work despite endemic skills shortages, their high levels of education, desire to earn a living, and legal right to work [in the EU] through the Temporary Protection Directive.'[63] Globally, there are 110 million people who have been forcibly displaced from their countries, people who need a helping hand. See The Tent Partnership for Refugees or the Breaking Barriers websites for advice on hiring refugees.

I am an Ambassador for Hope for Justice charity, whose aim is to end the modern-day slavery impacting over 50 million people globally, and have seen first-hand the work they do to stem the flow of people into slavery and rescue victims. Besides opening employment to a survivor, who may also be suffering homelessness, ensure that your company's supply chain is slave-free by joining the Slave-Free Alliance, a not-for-profit social enterprise launched by Hope for Justice.

Finally, look for inspirational leaders like Emma Freivogel, co-founder of Radical Recruit and charity B-Radical, who helps companies turn CSR, ESG, and Social Value commitments into meaningful actions by bridging the gap between disadvantaged job seekers and employment.

And always remember the proverb: *'there but for the grace of God go I.'*

Chapter Summary

- If you exclude people or make people feel uncomfortable; they'll write about the -isms and phobias they experienced, damaging both the employer brand and your personal brand.
- Everyone in your company's hiring process needs to demonstrate behaviours that align with any stated policies on DEIB, including third parties who act on your behalf.
- Diverse teams are 33% more likely to outperform on profitability, and 76% of job seekers look for a diverse workforce; it makes business sense to lose lingering -isms and phobias.

6

Interview Catalysts

Research from Randstad found that 53% of employees have left or considered leaving their jobs because they believe their employers don't recruit or retain high-performing individuals.[1] Let's reboot thinking about interviews and reduce the chance of this happening at your firm.

To manage expectations, you won't find a list of interview questions here or a guide on creating them; your talent acquisition partner can help you design them based on your brilliant articulation of the hiring need. In this chapter, I have focused on easy ways to improve interviews and the consequences of poor behaviour in a search-engine-led world. I have also argued for keeping technology in its rightful place: supporting humans.

Shortlisting

For years, I have thought that the biggest issue in recruitment happens because managers struggle to articulate who they need to hire. The attempt becomes a flawed job description, to which recruiters endeavour to match resumes – documents people find hard to write and are equally flawed. The better the recruitment alignment meeting, the more likely sourcing and advertising will attract suitable applicants. However, no matter how well done, bias starts creeping into the process at the assessing and matching phase, whether by humans or AI.

In a 2023 survey by Greenhouse, 19% of US respondents admitted to changing their names on their resumes when applying for a job; 45% to sound less ethnic, 42% to seem younger, and 22% to sound like the opposite gender.[2] Anecdotally, a Black British talent acquisition specialist confided that she can receive surprised looks when meeting someone for the first time because neither her accent nor her name gives any clues to her heritage. Both you and your talent acquisition partner may seek to combat such unconscious bias with technology, but is it any better?

A recent Bloomberg experiment testing ChatGPT's shortlisting capabilities, by asking it to compare equally qualified resumes using different made-up names, found that it consistently discriminated against African American men.[3] In the article detailing their research, 'OpenAI's GPT is a recruiter's dream tool. tests show there's racial bias', they added, 'After Bloomberg first got in touch with OpenAI in December to ask about the software's use in the hiring industry, the company updated those policies to say it prohibits use that makes "high-stakes automated decisions in domains that affect an individual's safety, rights or well-being, e.g., employment."'

Cynically, I doubt a policy tucked away in the terms and conditions will stop recruiters from using it to save time. The perception that Talent Acquisition is a cost centre places them under pressure to cut corners, and the buzz around Generative AI is immense, with few brave enough to voice concerns about the potential risks.

However, even if recruiters don't use ChatGPT in this manner, most applicant tracking systems use AI to parse applicants' resumes and provide rankings that help recruiters shortlist. On Hilke Schellmann's post, where I first saw the Bloomberg article, Alon Algai added, 'I've also been hearing (anecdotally) from recruiters that the enterprise AI-powered resume screeners are simply not doing a good job. High-score candidates aren't getting to the offer stage. My colleagues have started sifting through the low-score applications and finding highly viable candidates.' Hilke replied, 'I would love, love, love to see a study on how high-scoring candidates are not as well suited for the role as AI models suggest.'[4] She is correct; we need more research.

As Irish Talent Acquisition and Sourcing Professional Ivan Stojanovic quipped on LinkedIn, 'Today relying on AI to recruit for you is like turning a task over to an intern. They're hardworking and helpful. But they're also inexperienced and underpaid, so you better check their work.'[5] I couldn't agree more. Rather than rushing in, consider carefully where, when, and how your company incorporates AI into the hiring process, and for now, equip the team with the humans it needs to be effective.

Types of Interviews

In Chapter 1, I explained that you will agree on an interview loop with your talent acquisition partner during the recruitment alignment meeting. I also mentioned the importance of making interviews two-way and balanced. As promised, in this chapter, I will share tips and considerations to ensure you save time, money, and hassle.

Initial Screen

The screening call is usually the first conversation an applicant has with a company, commonly with a Talent Acquisition member – though some companies may rely on agency recruiters for this. The aim is to check that the applicant has the skills and abilities for the role, to discover if the salary meets expectations, to explain the hiring process, and to uncover the personal motivators prompting the change of employment. Recruitment and leadership coach Angela Cripps advises, 'Screening calls aren't just about identifying whether the candidate is capable of fulfilling the role, to move them forward in the process, it's also about identifying whether they will be a good advocate for your company.'

During the initial screen, Talent Acquisition can identify diamonds in the rough, highlight areas of concern for you to probe, and save you time, money, and hassle by ensuring you're not interviewing unsuitable people. But they cannot do this if you hold them at arm's length, refusing to partner and are reluctant to provide the necessary information.

Structured Interviews

Asking the same questions to all interviewees in the same order and scoring responses against objective criteria make responses comparable and the interview structured. Unlike unstructured interviews, which are free-flowing, they can help you avoid affinity bias, beauty bias, the halo effect, the horns bias, stereotyping, and the contrast effect because you will avoid delving into backgrounds and education, which may not be relevant to the role. Having multiple interviewers who assign scores independently can further reduce the likelihood of bias and improve assessment.

Structured interviews also save you time because you are not creating new questions for each interview. By using a pre-determined set of questions and scoring criteria, interviews are efficient, making applicant comparison easy and objective, which speeds up the decision-making process. Questions could be hypothetical work scenarios, case studies, or testing for skills in a job simulation or role-play. Importantly, although each interviewee answers the same questions in the same order, it is OK to ask follow-up questions if you need more information.

I hoped managers and leaders had moved on from asking brainteasers or questions that interviewers cannot rank equitably. However, according to American Talent Acquisition Director Jeff Shapiro's recent post, this has yet to happen. He wrote, 'If the Job-Seeking Human (AKA the candidate) can answer your question by saying, "What does that have to do with my ability to do the job?" — the question you're asking has little to no value.'[6] This post followed his previous one, 'Worst. Interview. Question. Ever. If you were a vegetable, what kind of vegetable would you be. . . and why?', a question introducing all manner of bias.[7]

Several people replied that they would think negatively of the interviewer and consider withdrawing from the process. Don't risk a costly restart; ensure you can equitably rate responses and avoid questions introducing prejudice.

Critically, give interviewees time to interview you, too. It can be wise to finish the structured part of the interview and move to something more conversational, led by their questions. Remember to genuinely sell the role and your company's mission and value.

Panels

Though the ultimate hiring decision belongs to you as the manager or leader, including your team in the hiring process makes sense, ensuring it represents diversity even more so. Your team offers a different perspective and will see things you won't do, due to your natural blind spots. It also makes the team feel valued, helps develop their interviewing skills, and means they will want the new hire to succeed because they were involved. For candidates, it can help their decision-making because they know who they will be working with, the culture, and so on.

However, consider the impact on the interviewee. Stephen Telford, a British Senior Talent Acquisition Specialist, wrote on LinkedIn:

> *These panel interviews are out of control. I recently spoke with someone interviewed for a job making 50k in front of ELEVEN people. He said it felt like he was up for public execution. For me, that's an inefficient company. If they can afford to take eleven people out for a couple of hours for each candidate, they're not in control of finances.*

To which Dan Cohen swiftly commented with, '11 people @ c.£40 / hour × 6 shortlisted candidates = £2,640 per stage. They must be rich!'[8]

Sometimes, panel numbers are inherited inefficiencies. I was mentoring a talent acquisition leader struggling to organise two five-person panels for every interviewee for the company she had recently joined. I asked her, 'Why so many? That's ridiculous!' As soon as she escalated the question and pointed out how inefficient it was, they dropped the second round, something introduced in the distant past that nobody had thought to query! Investing in training for all interviewers and dropping the excessive rounds will help save time, money, and hassle and improve the company's reputation with candidates.

Remember, also, that you want to avoid looking like your company has a blame culture. The more rounds and the greater the number of panellists in each round, the more it will look like employees are scared to decide lest it is wrong and they get into trouble. I recommend three people maximum in a panel, using a good structure to minimise the rounds so people don't withdraw.

Psychometric Tests

How many personality tests have you taken over the years? Did many describe you well? I have taken countless; few were anything like me. The only one I have ever found of value and freakily accurate was Gallup's CliftonStrengths, but then it isn't a personality test; it works to find out what someone is gifted at naturally. The test was also thorough and could not be gamed. However, I wouldn't want it used to decide if someone remained in a hiring process because it took a long time to complete, needed a certified assessor to explain, and would only be valid if the manager truly knew the strengths required for success in the role.

Psychometric tests measure interests, personality, and aptitude. The Chartered Institute of Personnel and Development (CIPD) advises, 'Evidence suggests that standardised tests or tests of cognitive ability can be good predictors of job performance, especially for occupations that require complex thinking, although test results should never be the sole basis for a selection decision.'[9] I would argue that it is unwise to use them as selection criteria at all.

In a post on Reddit, u/Reservedfornow perfectly describes the issue created by most personality tests: 'When I got the news that I needed to complete a personality test in order to advance to the next round of my dream job, I was already deeply worried. Especially considering I'm neurodivergent. I worry it will somehow sniff that out and label me unfavourably.'[10]

Later in the post, they say:

I feel confident in my work, am good at prioritising, communicating, and juggling many things. I've been very successful and have a good work/life balance. I will never know how questions such as the following are supposed to measure any of that, or maybe my way of thinking is just incompatible with these things. Examples: I a. am courteous with others or b. never panic; I relate more to a. feeling sad or b. embellishing the truth; I relate more to a. feeling low or b. feeling superior; I tend to a. keep to myself or b. avoid theoretical discussions. Anyway, I fully hated this process and feel so dejected and sad about losing this opportunity at the long-list phase of recruitment.

Feeling sad versus lying? Low versus superior? Most people will struggle with these questions and worry about automatic rejection. I wonder if the people who implemented it into the process had experienced the test. It seems unlikely, and I am sure they would hate knowing they were leaving applicants feeling dejected and sad.

In *The Guardian*'s 2021 article, reviewing the documentary *Persona: The Dark Truth Behind Personality Tests*, journalist Lisa Wong Macabasco wrote:

Today more than 2 million take the MBTI every year, including 60% to 70% of American prospective workers. All this despite the well-known facts that the MBTI has no grounding in clinical psychology (Jung's theories weren't drawn from controlled experiments or data either), its results are poorly correlated with job performance, and embedded within it are false and dangerous ideas about race, gender, and class that drive bias and discrimination.[11]

Wow, 60 to 70% of prospective workers! That is deeply concerning, especially as this only relates to the Myers-Briggs Type Indicator, not the countless other offerings used globally.

Unless you are entirely confident in defining the personality traits that guarantee job success and know without a doubt that the technology isn't flawed or biased, consider their use in culling applicants carefully. As the CIPD also advises,

Tests should be supported by a body of statistical evidence which demonstrates their validity and reliability. Most tests are developed by occupational psychologists and should be accompanied by detailed manuals that

explain how test scores should be used so that employers can compare their test candidates against benchmark scores of similar people (also known as a norm group). Administering tests and analysing the results is a skilled task and requires training and certification.

If your company still feels strongly about using psychometrics and testers are certified, instead of using tests to disqualify people from the hiring process, consider using them as part of onboarding. Ask the test-taker how they feel about the results, and together, decide if they could be useful as a guide to working together.

Use video assessment tools with caution, too. In 2019, concerns began about the algorithms behind HireVue. For the *MIT Technology Review*, Angela Chen wrote, 'The algorithm analyses video interviews, using everything from word choice to facial movements to figure out an "employability score" that is compared against that of other applicants.' She said the problem is that:

It's hard to predict which workers will be successful from things like facial expressions. Worse, critics worry that the algorithm is trained on limited data, and so will be more likely to mark "traditional" applicants (white, male) as more employable. As a result, applicants who deviate from the "traditional" — including people who don't speak English as a native language or who are disabled — are likely to get lower scores.[12]

On top of this bias, candidates can learn to game it; websites like Voomer coach job seekers in how to do this.

Thankfully, Will Knight reported for WIRED in 2021 that 'Hirevue is killing off a controversial feature of its software: analysing a person's facial expressions in a video to discern certain characteristics.' That was the right move, especially as psychologist and neuroscientist Lisa Feldman Barrett, PhD, said in the article, 'A person's face does not on its own reveal emotion or character.

Just by looking at someone smiling, you can't really tell anything about them except maybe that they have nice teeth. It is a bad idea to make psychological inferences and therefore determine people's outcomes based on facial data alone.'[13]

If you are considering implementing any form of test, assessment, or game to remove people from the applicant list, especially without any form of appeal process, read Hilke Schellman's book, *The Algorithm: How AI Can Hijack Your Career and Steal Your Future*.[14] It is thoroughly researched and will help you make the right move for your company and current and future employees.

Skill-Based Assessments

Assessing interviewees through relevant work sample tasks, situational judgement tests, simulations, or assessment centres are better predictors of job performance than traditional approaches such as reviewing job experience, education, or unstructured interviews. They can be conducted during an interview or as online tests.

TestGorilla, one company offering candidate-friendly online skills tests, has a library of tests including languages, software and programming skills, role-specific skills, situational judgement, and even typing speed. It integrates with most applicant tracking systems and has built-in benchmarking so candidate results can be compared to scores achieved by existing employees.

As someone who hates the timed tests on Duolingo, as I attempt to learn French for the fourth time, I was curious to know what accommodations are made for those who take longer to read questions, among other things. João Magalhães, TestGorilla's social media maestro, said:

Before a candidate starts an assessment, we ask them if they have a condition such as dyslexia, ADD, ADHD or other condition that may affect memory and concentration abilities and send an accommodated version in under 24 hours. We ensure they know their request is private but will be asked if they would like to inform the employer; it is optional. If they choose to, we do not provide details; we only inform the employer that we gave an accommodation.

When completing any tests, candidates will appreciate knowing the length of the test, an outline of what to expect, that you are open to making reasonable adjustments and that they don't impact decision-making, how you use the tests in the hiring process, and feedback to help them grow – unlike the example I share a little later! Also, avoid tarnishing the company's employer brand and future hiring ability by asking applicants to complete a test or assignment that takes more than a few hours. If you insist on using lengthy assignments, pay them for their time and reassure them that it isn't a guise to collect free work and strategies.

Finally, place the test after a conversation with the applicant. u/Charming-Plastic-679 shared on Reddit in February 2024, 'I applied for a software engineering job on LinkedIn, and without having any communication with the company whatsoever, no calls, emails, interviews, nothing, I get an invite for a technical test that they estimate should take only 71 minutes.'[15] The comments were an array of don't bother, had similar at [company name], and worse. So be sure to save everyone's time, money, and hassle, and don't let the test be the first response someone receives from your company.

Assessment Centres

Assessment days tend to be held in person, and candidates work individually or in groups on various exercises, including activities like case studies, group discussions, presentations, psychometrics, written tests, role plays, or social events.

In Chapter 1, I mentioned the workshop I delivered for a new veterinary practice and the leaders' startling realisation that time was limited. The only way to meet the opening deadline was through recruitment open days; delivered by the team at Never Mind The Job Spec. Their lead Talent Acquisition Project Manager Glenn Martin said:

> *The days commenced with a meet and greet to ensure people felt calm, then moved to communication, collaboration, data or problem analysis, prioritisation and decision-making assessments, and a tour of the unique features of the new veterinary practice. The day ended with Ask Me Anything sessions, focusing on answering all the candidates' questions because transparency is the key to engagement and retention.*

Importantly, candidates were well informed before the day via emails and welcome packs with videos walking through the agenda and assessments; this also gave the team time to make any reasonable adjustments when requested. Afterwards, feedback was gathered from all participants so that the team could change future days using their test, analyse, iterate, and deploy methodology. Overall, attendees said that the day was unexpected for all the right reasons, and they left enthusiastic about the opportunity to join the practice.

Interview Prep

Before any interview, re-read the screening summary from your Talent Acquisition partner and note any areas of concern they would like you to probe. As crazy as this might sound, be sure you know who you will be interviewing so you start by delivering a positive impression.

Accessibility and Inclusivity

In 2022, the team at Personio invited me to run a seminar at their Hug On Tour London event. I suggested a design-thinking workshop because it is a great way to include everyone and ensure even the shy ones are heard. On the day, I was excited to see who would join in, and I was ready to deliver what I thought was an experience suitable for all. Then Isaac Harvey MBE wheeled in, and I immediately knew my perception of inclusion was riddled with ableism! Thankfully, he brought a friend who could be his scribe and appreciated my openness. He also said something I have not forgotten, 'You moved the chair; you'd be stunned how few facilitators think to do that!'

At every point, consider whether the interview is accessible to all, and always offer reasonable adjustments that make the process fair and equitable. Be that with Recite Me accessibility software on your website and career site, handing out the interview questions in advance, physically making changes to include people with neurodivergence or disabilities, and many more.

Last-Minute Cancellations

There are few legitimate excuses for creating a scenario like this, 'I had an interview get cancelled on me literally 15 minutes before start time. I was in the lobby of the building. What made it worse was that I came in from out of town. Travelled almost 3 hours to make it to the lobby.'[16] How would you feel about a 6-hour pointless round trip? Besides the lost hours, how much would you have spent on fuel or transport? Would you have organised child or pet care and used annual leave to attend the interview? What emotions would you be expressing in that lobby? I know my anger and frustration would be palpable.

Besides being unkind and disrespectful, last-minute cancellations damage your personal reputation, employer brand, and future hiring and are mostly avoidable. Agree to a contingency plan in the recruitment alignment meeting; decide who can interview in your place, and if absolutely nobody else can, it is better that you, as the interviewer, deliver the news and reschedule.

German Talent Acquisition Manager Nadine Hofschneider said:

> *I always discuss the impact of cancellations in conversations with my managers and leaders, and we set the rules of the game; they know to keep their calendars maintained. We agree that if an interview is booked with an applicant and cancelled by the manager, the manager reschedules the interview. This agreement and respect have significantly reduced the number of cancellations and improved the hiring experience for all.*

Take 5

Have you ever walked into a room and just known the people in the room were fighting? Though they weren't speaking as you entered, you could just tell. As energetic beings, we can sense other people's energy; it is intrinsic, and we use it to stay safe. Before any interview, in-person or online, take a few slow, deep breaths to centre and calm to avoid giving the wrong impression to your candidate.

During the Interview

In Chapter 5, I shared the -isms and phobias that can rear their ugly heads in interviews; you may have even been appalled. Here, I want to discuss a few more behaviours that can make an interviewee uncomfortable and unwilling to proceed.

Be Punctual

Not only be on time but turn up! Something is unsettling about waiting for a video call to commence when people are late. Questions race, panic rises as you wonder if you are using the correct link, and time seems twice as long as you stare into the abyss. Do your utmost to be on time by avoiding back-to-back meetings and placing non-negotiable time padding around interview slots. Of course, tardiness is still poor etiquette for in-person meetings, but hopefully, you can send someone to inform them of the wait. Always apologise for any delays to avoid damaging your and your employer's reputation.

Take a few moments to settle the candidate into the interview. In-person, that happens during the small talk from reception to the interview room; online, that happens by asking if they expect any interruptions, can hear and see you OK, feel ready, etc. Do this before launching into the questioning.

Be Present and Prepared

You don't need to read Johann Hari's book, *Stolen Focus: Why You Can't Pay Attention—And How to Think Deeply Again*, to know that we now struggle to concentrate, though I highly recommend that you do because it is eye-opening.[17] However, not being present, ready, and interested because your mind is focused on other things will signal to candidates that you are not interested in them and could force you to start the entire hiring cycle again.

Fatigue

With 21 years of recruitment industry experience, I'll confess that until I heard about Gabrielle Judge's viral TikTok,

I had never made a correlation between an exhausted interviewer and a potential lack of work-life balance. In it, she says that one of the things she looks for is if the interviewer is tired or unprepared, as this could signal that they are overworked or the company has had a recent lay-off.[18]

Even when feeling healthy and rested, interviewer fatigue happens from the repetition, the effort required to be present and actively listen, too many back-to-back interviews, constant monitoring for biases, the stress of keeping interviews on time, the pressure of the decision, etc. Unfortunately, the candidates will suffer if you are tired, so endeavour to limit the number of interviews each day to three or four and schedule plenty of breaks to decompress and refresh.

Ditch the Grill

Awkwardly, I found this review while preparing a workshop with a new client. The interviewee wrote, 'The second interview was with three different managers. It was a BBQ, and I was on the menu. None of them even cracked a smile or seemed interested in having the interview with me. I'm pretty sure one manager was replying to emails during the meeting, as he did not seem present at all.' Though the reviewer praised the HR team, I found their initial response when I shared this review with them surprising; they blamed the candidate until I pointed out there was more than one.

It is no longer the 1990s; people won't accept a grilling or disinterest. It is possible to keep a professional distance while making an interviewee feel welcome and comfortable.

Don't Lie!

As I mentioned in Chapter 4, lies are costly. Someone starting on false pretences and promptly leaving impacts more than the bottom line. I believe as AI continues to infiltrate our lives, we will crave the truth and reality. No job or company is perfect; let them choose you and your company because you were refreshingly frank about the realities.

Video Etiquette

Desperately, I was trying to find a post about the discomfort a senior software engineer experienced when two managers refused to turn their cameras on in a video interview, but sadly, there are now so many similar posts I couldn't find this one in the pile. To surmise, though, to deliver an experience that keeps people in the hiring process, all parties have their cameras on, or all parties have them off, with no exceptions; it is an interview, not an inquisition. This applies to your talent acquisition partner, too – though, when asked, applicants often admit they prefer an initial call to a video screen.

However, I found another post perfectly illustrating why using care and consideration with video technology is essential. This complaint features regularly in forums, too. In March 2024, u/livvykitty14 wrote on Reddit's Recruiting Hell, 'He [hiring manager] says I'll build rapport by doing a one-way recorded video interview.' She included redacted screenshots of the email exchange in the post.[19]

The first email from the manager beautifully explains the hiring process, which commences with a one-way video. He explains the time required, offers tips and is positive. This is good, but it is before the applicant has had an opportunity to check the basics. U/livvykitty14 replies with empathy and awareness that the manager is acting as both manager and recruiter, explaining that a two-way interview would create better rapport. She wrote, 'It is distracting speaking at yourself to a camera without any opportunity to prepare for the prompts' and asked for a 15-minute two-way distraction-free interview. [Though not mentioned, I wondered about neurodiversity at this point; this adjustment request was reasonable.]

His response, 'This stand is perplexing. The video responses are the same questions I would ask everyone in an early stage screen round and are designed specifically for the candidate to build a rapport.' Now, I am perplexed, too. I have 13 years of experience delivering straight to the camera for training, webinars, etc., and it is hard! It is like talking to the wall. Who are they building rapport with, the camera? And think how often you look at yourself on a regular video call; it is distracting.

As one commenter said, 'To be fair – this is a perfect screening tool. For companies I would NOT want to work at, that is.' This sentiment is the crux of the matter; HR tech vendors sell these tools as the solution to all your hiring woes. However, if applicants don't like them or don't find them inclusive and withdraw, you lose the opportunity to hire a potentially great new employee.

Tips for Novice Interviewers

For all my experience, I have not had to coach novice interviewers, so I crowdsourced some advice for you from my global talent acquisition network.

Manuel Vargas, a Costa Rican Talent Acquisition Director, always shares these three things with his new interviewing managers:

> *Have an open mind and watch for biases; interview your first candidates beyond what you read on their CV. Add some structure to the interview with a logical order of questions, which will also help with the duration of the session and ensure time for the interviewee's questions. Lastly,*

make sure they feel comfortable in your environment, make eye contact, and use a pace and tone of voice that sounds less like an inquisition and more like a conversation.

Similarly, Dutch Global Head of Talent Acquisition Bianca Eder coaches her managers to do the following:

Make the interview flow back and forth, inspire each other, don't just ask the interviewee to go through their CV. Discuss your vision, your love for your job, and how you plan to achieve strategic goals. If you talk to them about relevant things, for example, 'I was looking into this tool for [task], what do you think of it?' it will help you connect with their past experiences and discover where they want to go.

Hire People Better Than You

Bianca added that it is crucial to do the following:

Know your current team's skills, knowledge, and attitudes. Then, work out what you are missing and what you will need to achieve your goals. You need the rule breakers, the analytical, the process-driven, the in- and out-of-the-box thinkers, and a team that gets on with it. Hire someone better than you, who is not afraid of making mistakes – and you, as their leader, don't be afraid to stand up and support them when they make them. That's your duty.

On International Women's Day, my friend Louise Triance wrote in a post, 'At Crowdcast, I have dream colleagues, including Melissa Hayes, who is evidence that you should hire people who are better than you!' She explained:

In areas where our roles overlap, she has more experience, produces higher quality written work and is more focused. Perhaps if I was concerned about my job security, I may have been tempted to hire a poor performer to make myself look better. Instead, I hired her because she is great for the role, and I knew I would learn lots!

After the Interviews

As mentioned in Chapter 1, your next steps will hopefully be to make an offer and have it accepted, or to kindly and compassionately displace the unsuccessful people. Closing everyone is essential to creating a positive candidate experience, but it must never be like the example below. Never ever!

A Lesson in Rejection

In Recruiting Hell on Reddit, u/iam014 shared the 'aggressive rejection email' Elite Automation Software sent to their friend.[20] The post has received 20,000 upvotes and 4000 comments in the last two months alone. It is also doing the rounds on LinkedIn and Blind and is visible in the press via the News tab on Google.

After being thanked for their application, the rejection email says, underlined for emphasis, '<u>Your job application for the Frontend Software Engineer position has been DECLINED</u>.' Then, without underline, 'due to your failed score on the automated online test, as you have scored below the pass score'. Fair enough, but the company adds, 'Please do not attempt to take the test again.' And for emphasis, this time in bold red, '**Do not attempt to apply again for this position until at least after the end of next year.**' Then they add, '**Any repeated attempts to apply** for this position again before this time, or any attempts to retake the test will lead to an automated decline of your application, as well as a **permanent blacklisting** [I am quoting verbatim; I apologise if this insensitive term causes offence] of your profile from any further applications.'

It continues with more threats of blocking, lack of empathy and insults, including:

If you are upset by this email, we have to inform you that life is hard and that part of any professional or personal development is dealing with rejection and finding ways to improve. You were provided an opportunity to show your abilities in a blind and fair test that is the same for all candidates, and that focused on nothing but skills and abilities. You have failed to score high enough on this test. Instead of blaming us, you should examine what you can do to improve those abilities and skills. Maybe you could use this self-reflection to improve and make your life better. We certainly wish the best for you.

It is signed by the 'Team at Elite Software Automation.'

It is breathtakingly and unnecessarily harsh; I have not seen a ruder rejection email in two decades. It made me curious about the company's legitimacy and the leader's character.

The technology for the test is from TestDome. Their site displays a case study from Elite Software Automation where the CEO states, 'My business is to transform other people's businesses. It requires extremely intelligent and straight-thinking people, who make up less than .5% of the workforce. Most people who work in consulting are good at presenting and selling themselves but completely suck at delivering.'[21] It would be easy as a consultant to be offended by such a sweeping statement, but I will ignore it.

The case study continues, 'To speed up his hiring process, Mykola [the CEO] created a pre-screening test in Test-Dome for each open position.' It ends, 'With TestDome, Mykola can screen 1,500 candidates a month by himself — eliminating the need for an HR team. Mykola says, "The value of TestDome has far exceeded the cost." He estimates that while he has spent more than $50,000 on TestDome this year, hiring a small HR team would have cost him as much as $500,000.'

The cynic in me wonders if any unknown company with fewer than 50 employees and minimal social media presence receives 1500 software engineer applicants monthly, especially when advertisements use wording like, 'WARNING! This is a position for experienced advanced level developers with commercially operating practical development experience ONLY. We do not accept juniors, entry-level, or interns. We will not even entertain requests by any juniors to work for free or less pay. Do not bother reaching out with requests like this; they will all be denied.'[22, 23] I will spare you the rest, but it includes threats of being blocked again.

Ample evidence of the CEO's leadership style is visible online with minimal digging. First is the addition to the company's career site about this Reddit thread, which claims it was 'sparked by an out-of-context screenshot of a rejection email received by one of the candidates in the hiring process.'[24] Then there are the replies to the negative – yet suspiciously 5-star – reviews on Glassdoor that reinforce the wording from the viral Reddit post and job advertisements.[25] Finally, there is the paid *Business Insider* press release, which starts, 'Not Intimidated by Social Media Outrage' and states. 'Many seasoned industry experts have already passed it and joined the highly coveted Elite Software Automation spots, just like many less experienced, less driven, and debatably less skilled individuals failed in doing so.'[26] I am agape; how does failing a test indicate someone is less experienced or less driven?

So, though US-based Elite Software Automation believes it saved $500,000, I wonder about the cost to the company's reputation as a service provider and an employer; the email even made it into *India Times*.[27] From within the

Reddit comments, I can see that users actively targeted the company's Google listing, reducing it to 1 star – I cannot fact-check this, though, because the Google Business page is no longer visible, which won't be great for the company's search engine optimisation or branding.

Perhaps the job wording has been written from frustration that people without the relevant skills apply, but that is simply part of hiring. Maybe the rejection email isn't meant to humiliate, but there is little need to be superior and unkind to people who have invested their irreplaceable time completing a technical test. As a service-providing company, the behaviour is surprising; the internet provides transparency, and the impact of this post will linger. It will deter clients and future employees.

However, I shared this because many companies will attempt to replace Talent Acquisition with technology, and lessons can be learned.

- Though a test may seem like a logical first step, highly sought-after talent is unlikely to apply without knowing the salary or contract rate.
- Instead of humiliating anyone who fails, build them up. For example, 'We know our test is hard; the pass rate is 85%. Those who passed said they studied here [insert appropriate training/school]; they could be worth a look. Thank you again for taking the test!'
- Being unkind will likely lead to a damaging viral online post; job seeking is emotionally taxing enough without belittling applicants with insults and aggression.
- The advice of a talent acquisition professional and a compassionate rejection email will prevent the loss of future employees and clients.

Swift Feedback

German-based Leadership Coach and HR Professional Gary Griffith added, 'Everyone loses if you delay interview feedback: the candidate, company, and team members. Delays in hiring usually mean the team, shouldering the extra workload, feels pressure to pick up the slack to ensure productivity, and that can lead to poorer quality because everyone is exhausted, or worse, people end up sick and absent. So keep the hiring process moving!'

In Chapter 4, I mentioned that 87% of applicants become down or depressed when they don't receive feedback. Your talent acquisition team, caught in the middle, also suffers if they don't obtain or only receive poor-quality feedback; displacing candidates becomes unnecessarily taxing and tarnishes their reputation. However, giving them constructive feedback should be relatively easy if you conduct fair and structured interviews with scorecards. Swift delivery will also allow for a revised search using the new information.

For interviewees, the emotional peak in the hiring process is usually in the interview, while the end is a generic email advising that their application was unsuccessful. Using this peak-end rule, Australia's NSW Government ran an experiment to increase the number of women reapplying after they narrowly missed out on a role.[28] Unlike men, women were unlikely to reapply for a senior role within six months and would doubt their skills. To counter this, a recruitment manager emailed and called each applicant to tell them how well they had done and to encourage them to reapply. The result was a 27% increase in the likelihood of women reapplying for a senior role and a reduction of the gender gap between men and women reapplying from 45%

to just 4%. Using this principle is a great way to reengage silver medallists, particularly minority candidates.

Don't Sit on Offers

U/Asleep-Inspection747 shared on Reddit, 'After accepting the offer from Company A, I reached out to the recruiter from Company B to let her know that I appreciated her time, as well as everyone else's that I had spoken to, but that I was withdrawing my application.'[29] He outlines the reasons for the decision – remote work and a shorter commute – and mentions how many interviews Company B had cancelled at the last minute. Later, he receives a text from her manager, whom he has never spoken to, that 'felt very unprofessional and strange, and the wording rubbed me the wrong way.'

The text said:

> *We would almost 100% come in with a higher offer as well as the scope for you would be much more compelling vs anything else out there, especially in the Atlanta area. I want to respect your decision but also push back a bit and let you know that the decision to withdraw was probably a bit premature. We can even get you onsite today. The team was just super pumped about you.*

Almost 100%? More compelling? Suddenly, it's onsite today? This message sounds desperate and hollow because of its delivery via text, the lack of rapport, and the insufficient knowledge of the candidate's personal motivators, which may not be money or scope. It reinforced that he had made the right choice, and it damaged the employer brand.

Thinking someone will wait for your job offer is a surefire way to restart the hiring process, so don't delay it. Throughout the process it is critical to discover the applicant's drivers so that when you do make that swift offer, you can meet their needs and make it easy for them to say yes.

Metrics That Matter

As you have read, many elements of this process are in your control as the person hiring for the position. However, this also means there are many spots where busy and stressed managers and leaders can create roadblocks and delays, make the process less effective, and increase stress for all parties, impacting reputations and future hiring. Yet, in most organisations, the most common measures for recruitment are time-to-hire and cost-per-hire, metrics outside of Talent Acquisition's full control.

As French Talent Acquisition Leader Thibault Martin perfectly explained in a recent post:

> *Does time-to-fill really matter if the person isn't a cultural fit? Does cost-per-hire really matter if the person leaves after six months? Yes, we need data to guide and measure our efforts, but let's not forget about quality. Measure this: waiting time between interview stages, submission-to-hire conversion rate, satisfaction rate among new hires, and retention rate during the first year. Let's make HR metrics. . . human again.*[30]

Pre- and Onboarding

Preboarding is the time between an accepted offer and someone's first day. However, just because someone signs your employment contract doesn't mean they will turn up on day one. They could still be receiving approaches, and if they feel neglected, they could be tempted away, leaving you to start the entire process again. You may also recall that

I shared in Chapter 3 that companies with an onboarding programme retain 58% of employees for three years, and 77% of new hires hit their first performance milestone.

Successful pre- and onboarding is a team effort between you, Talent Acquisition, and Human Resources. However, if you don't want to restart the entire hiring process and want to take the pressure off your team by ensuring this new hire starts and succeeds, invest in and actively participate in a pre- and onboarding programme.

In my book, *The Robot-Proof Recruiter*, I share a chapter of tips, stories and examples to help your Talent Acquisition and Human Resources team stop non-boarding. I also share Talent Acquisition's favourite onboarding technology for taking the load off this process, especially for managers and leaders, which includes Enboarder, SmarterMedium PerStart, Eloomi and Appical. These companies also share plenty of information and case studies to help you ensure that you don't waste all of the time, money, and energy you invested in the hiring process with a failed start.

Chapter Summary

- Inherently biased humans create and feed the AI in HR technology; relying on it alone to screen, shortlist, or knock out applicants is unwise.
- Similarly, psychometric tests should be used cautiously and not to rule people out; relevant skill-based assessments are more accurate.
- Keep tests until after an applicant has had initial communication with Talent Acquisition and always cater to reasonable adjustments.

- Structured interviews give the fairest assessment; include the team but cap the number at three to avoid intimidating the interviewee. Let the interviewee ask questions!
- Poor behaviour before, during, and after interviews irreversibly damages personal reputations and the employer brand, making future hiring harder.
- Displace people from the process with kindness, compassion, and decent feedback.
- Don't delay offers without cause; get involved with pre- and onboarding, or you may need to start over.

7

The Hiring Benefits
of Getting Social

An attitude of "I don't do social media" creates problems when you are hiring for your team. It isn't a valid excuse, nor a reason to skip this chapter, because though you may not "do" social media, 93.5% of internet users do.[1] Missing or poorly completed profiles hinder the attraction and retention of employees and even clients. (It might be limiting your career, too!)

In fact, in a recent LinkedIn poll, 89% of respondents said that before an interview, they find and look at the managers' profiles themselves, 3% receive it from the recruiter, and 1% look at profiles on other sites.[2] So, I hope to persuade you to 'do social media' a little better.

Don't worry; I don't want you to be the next TikTok influencer or spend hours daily immersed in Instagram! But I do recommend fixing some basics, making a tiny effort, and reading about managers and leaders who have used their social channels for hiring.

It Goes Both Ways

Recruiting in a talent-scarce industry, South African Sourcer and Trainer Vanessa Raath shared that candidates hesitate when the future manager doesn't have an online presence. 'They have choice, and it takes undue effort to persuade these candidates to continue because it can seem like the managers are not proud to work at their company. Not having a LinkedIn profile might be OK at a company with a desirable employer brand, but for most companies, it is only damaging.' She added, 'Insisting that your employees anonymise their place of work on LinkedIn, thinking this will somehow stop your team from being headhunted, also creates doubt in candidates. It's also pointless; recruiters will approach them anyway! It's better to create a work environment they don't want to leave.'

American Talent Attraction Specialist Derek Murphy-Johnson told me when he was last hiring for the C-suite, 'The CEO had a great background, but he was older and didn't use any social media; the absence of profile came up from applicants so frequently during the recruiting process, that I had to create one!' Australian Recruiter and Remote Work and Disability Advocate Hilary Callaghan also shared that they had to use every trick in the book to get their CTO to engage.

He was the 'star hire,' bringing in over a decade's experience in FAANG, which the start-up hoped would help attract 100 engineers in 8 months. We hoped to use his profile to attract people, but it was sparse; he had few connections and wasn't motivated to fix it. I joked I'd set up a reward system, and quite unexpectedly, getting his first gold star motivated him to increase his network and post content. His increased visibility and activity helped our hiring immensely.

Author of *Job Search Guide: Be Your Own Career Coach*, Jan Tegze, recommends that job seekers research target companies to ensure they are a cultural fit and suitable for their professional development. Among the interview preparation advice, he says, 'Company culture is often set by the CEO, executives, and senior vice presidents', and on top of ensuring interviewees meet them during the hiring process, he suggests, 'Check their LinkedIn profiles to see their perspectives on the company and what is going on there at the moment.' Further on, he adds, 'Research interviewers by looking at their LinkedIn profiles and the comments and articles they've shared or liked; you can get a sense of what is important to them professionally.'[3]

Finally, even if applicants don't seek out your social footprint, recruiters and talent acquisition professionals like to send LinkedIn profiles to interviewees so they can prepare for the conversation; it is excellent for employer branding and a wise step to improve the candidate experience. Because the internet shows other jobs and possibilities, future recruits don't have to choose you and your role, so help them make the decision easier by amping up your online presence. It is good for talent attraction and your career, too.

Bang on Basics

Let's give your future employees and clients, for that matter, something interesting to read by completing your profile basics. Primarily, I am focusing on LinkedIn because it is considered the largest professional network, recently surpassing 1 billion users after 20 years, but many suggestions could carry over to other professional networking sites, like Xing. Of LinkedIn users, millennials comprise 60% of account holders and, at the time of writing, are aged 28–43. Globally, 20% of users are aged 18–24, 18% are between 35 and 54, with just 2% of users over 55.[4]

Note Before you change an existing profile, you can avoid updates being announced to your connections by turning this feature off. In Settings & Privacy, which you will find in the dropdown menu under Me at the top right on the web version, head to Visibility. Under 'Visibility of your LinkedIn activity', turn off 'Share profile updates with your network'. Once off, you can make changes without receiving hundreds of mistaken 'congrats on the new job' comments, for example. While in the Visibility section, you may also want to turn off the Active status so people don't know when you're using the site.

Profile Photos

In a 2018 study, psychology researchers found that people make snap judgements of others based on their facial appearance and their preexisting beliefs about how personalities work. For example, if someone believes that competence and friendliness co-occur in people's personalities, then they will perceive the signals that make a face look competent and those that make a face look friendly as similar.[5] In other words, we all judge faces differently. Something to remember if you spy on candidate's profiles before interviews!

As their potential boss or leader, candidates will look at your profile photo to assess your competence and likeability. But if we all read faces differently, which picture do you use? Thankfully, sites like Photofeeler can help. In addition to offering lots of advice on what makes a great photo, you can upload a profile picture to have it judged by real people for business, social, or dating use. My current photo, rated by 20 strangers, received 8.2 for competency, 7.9 for likeability, and 8.4 for influence, each out of 10, so I am reassured it is a good choice for business.

If you plan to use multiple social media platforms, you may want to use the same profile photo across sites so people can find you through a reverse image search. Of course, if you don't want people to see your other profiles, don't do that! However, if you have an unusual name like mine, Google reveals everything. I just removed my photo and hid my name on Trustpilot lest I be perceived poorly for writing a few recent negative reviews.

Something to note: LinkedIn's default setting for profile photos is first-level connections, which means only those you are connected to can see your photo. Head to your profile and click on your picture to set it to 'everyone'. On the bottom left, you will notice an eye symbol; clicking it shows the visibility options.

On LinkedIn, you can add a purple #Hiring banner to your photo. Plus, if you can access LinkedIn Recruiter, you can even link your job vacancy to it. You may also have seen the green #OpenToWork banner, which polarises people. The bias is shocking when the 2020s have been a roller-coaster for far too many people globally due to the pandemic, poor workforce planning, and overhiring. Layoffs happen to good people; the banner helps them stand out and find new work sooner.

Banner Images

Your banner image is an opportunity to inject some personality into your profile. Your corporate communications or marketing team may have one they would prefer you use, but you can generally choose your own. The optimal image dimensions are 1584×396 pixels.

Give people something to talk to you about, something interesting to use as an icebreaker. CEO of Kyte Alice Ferrari does this perfectly.[6] Kyte empowers airlines with the next generation of retail tools, and though Alice could have used the corporate banner on her LinkedIn profile, she didn't. Instead, she chose a photo of two nose-diving planes, which immediately evokes a reaction. I even dropped my head sideways to view the image!

Headline

Your headline is visible when you comment and share a post; it appears in the preview on an invitation to connect and under 'who has viewed your profile'. You may simply choose to use your job title, but it can also be a place to express some personality and stand out. If you are hiring, you could mention that there, too. Pavlos Linos does this succinctly, 'CEO at Exit Bee – Hiring'.[7] Pavlos also chose a banner image that clearly states the company's mission, which is alluring to any passing job seeker.

On my profile, I have managed to squeeze 'Solving The Recruitment Problems AI Won't Fix | Facilitator & Speaker | Author: Reboot Hiring & The Robot-Proof Recruiter | | Memoirist: The Damage of Words | Podcast Host' into my headline. However, when I comment on a post, for example, only 'Solving The Recruitment Problems AI Won't Fix | Facilitator & S. . .' shows on the web version and just 'Solving The Recruitment Problems AI Won't Fix' on the app. So, be sure to create an impact with the first five to six words you choose because people may not click through to see the rest.

Also, if you plan to send invitations to connect without adding an explanation, ensure your headline isn't cryptic. I'm sure you have also accepted an unexplained invite from someone using a headline that sheds little light on who they are or what they do, only to receive a sales pitch a few moments later and wished you'd hit ignore!

Pronouns

As leaders in multi-generational workforces, you may have to set aside your personal beliefs to protect your reputation, employees, productivity, and the bottom line. The world is changing, and the young are leading the charge. Pew Research found in 2022 in the US that 5.1% of adults under 30 are trans or nonbinary, compared to just .3%

over 50. Though overall reported numbers are low, more than 44% of survey respondents also said they personally know someone who is trans, and 20% know someone who is non-binary.[8] Living in London, UK, I personally know at least ten openly trans and non-binary people ranging in age from 30 to 60, living around the world, and I probably missed someone!

In countries where being a member of the LGBTQIA+ community is legal, you are most likely to see the use of pronouns in communication and on social media profiles. If you are serious about building a diverse and inclusive team, your use of pronouns builds trust, affirms their identity, reduces depression, shows you are an ally, and helps a future employee think they could belong in your company. Most social media platforms allow the option of adding pronouns, and you will often see variants including she/her, he/him, they/them, ze/zir and more, or a combination like she/they. Senior Director of Talent Acquisition Alia Khattab added hers in multiple languages: (She/ه/Elle). Some people may ask you only to use their name. You may also find titles denoted there; I added Ms because I was tired of receiving assumptions about my marital status. Identity matters!

To add yours on LinkedIn, head to your profile and click the pencil under your banner image. A box will pop up, and a short scroll down will reveal the option to 'enter custom pronouns'.

Name Pronunciation

I'll confess, I thought saying Katrina Collier was easy, but I now know better, having been introduced on stages on five continents. Even emcees in other English-speaking countries have delivered some amusing mispronunciations, especially of my surname. So, I was grateful to have been able to add an audio recording of my name to LinkedIn when the pronunciation option appeared a few years ago.

While you are editing your profile, add a sound bite of your name. The recording is a great way to let people know how you prefer they say it and can instil confidence in interviewees.

About Section

The first thing someone sees on your profile is the About Section. It is your opportunity to share more about your experience, introduce yourself, and share some personality. There are no rules, so if you are an emoji fan, like me, throw some in.

Hubspot's article, '17 best LinkedIn summary & bio examples',[9] suggests writing it as follows:

- Hook: to encourage people to hit 'see more'.
- Mission: why do you do what you do?
- Expertise and skills: what are you good at?
- Accomplishments: how has your expertise delivered results in the past?
- Call to Action: what do you want the reader to do when they've read this?

On their website, Hubspot also has a fill-in-the-blanks free download of 80+ Professional Bio Examples & Templates, which I highly recommend and will be used to rewrite mine shortly. However, I dislike the third person examples for your LinkedIn profile; I think they look better in the first person. It's your profile, after all!

Like your Headline, LinkedIn only shows part of the About section before the reader must hit 'see more'; on the mobile app, that is about 30 words. Below is a taster of one of Hubspot's suggestions; it would create an impactful opening for any manager's or leader's About Section and appeal to future team members.

As a [Job Title], I oversee____, ____, and ____. I'm mainly involved with ____ and ____, as my primary goal is to ____.

I bring over [Number] years of experience to my role, including experience working with ____, ____, and ____. As a result of this background, my approach is very ____, and I bring a high level of ____ to the work.

You can download the rest and all examples at bit.ly/ HubSpot-LI-examples (case-sensitive).

Featured

At the time of writing, users who have switched on Creator mode can add a Featured Section to spotlight information or achievements. Here, you could highlight any presentations you have given or podcasts you have been on. You could add a link to your career site or upload a photo of your team (with permission). It is also possible to emphasise posts and articles. For example, I am currently highlighting my podcast, my book, *The Robot-Proof Recruiter*, and my memoir, *The Damage of Words*. This book will take pride of place there on its publication.

Activity

As Jan Tegze suggests to job seekers, the Activity Section is where potential recruits can get a sense of who you are by seeing your recent posts, the comments you make on other posts, those you react to, and so on. LinkedIn separates these into posts, comments, images, articles, newsletters, events, and documents, and you can choose what they see first by clicking the pencil. For example, anyone perusing my profile sees my newsletter first in this section.

In addition to sharing the job you are recruiting for, share posts that teach your network something or celebrate an achievement like company growth, a milestone, or an anniversary. If you have delivered a talk or webinar, you could cut the video into short videos and share those. And, of course, your marketers will love it if you repost and comment on anything they share on your company's LinkedIn page. Conscious that your time is precious, I have shared some quick post ideas later in this chapter.

A word of caution: on too many occasions, I have been stunned by the behaviour of LinkedIn users who forget that their profiles connect to their employers and that comments are public and remain visible on their profiles. Over the years, I have seen replies on posts displaying all manner of -isms, with the author forgetting that these remarks can be screenshot and sent to their employer. As managers and leaders, just as I hope you would "in the office", please consider the impact of your comments and don't post without due care. Sometimes, it is better just to keep scrolling.

Also, as tempting as employing an AI-commenting tool might be, thinking it will remove the effort of being active, the repetitive comments it posts on your behalf will appear in this section and not aid your personal brand. I finally blocked someone who employed an AI tool that commented on every single one of my posts because, though it helped my posts' visibility, I found the comments banal and inauthentic and thought less of this person.

Hopefully, these few warnings won't put you off being more active. Sharing content and engaging in conversations can attract candidates to your company and open unexpected possibilities for you.

Experience

This section is a reverse chronological order of your professional experience and often looks like someone's resume. Just like I mentioned in Chapter 2, resumes are hard to write, and so is the Experience Section. How do you share your knowledge without sounding like you have an inflated ego? How do you express confidence but not look cocky? Easy! Think, 'So what?' My excellent manager, Ray Murphy, shared that gem with me in my recruitment agency days, and it has served me well ever since.

Read through each line of your resume or experience section, thinking, 'So what?' and add the benefit or achievement. For example, 'Read Reboot Hiring', so what? 'Read Reboot Hiring, implemented the advice, which improved my recruitment alignment meetings and hired five recruits with minimal time, money, or stress.' Another example might be, 'Partnered with Talent Acquisition for hiring', 'So what?' 'Partnered with Talent Acquisition for hiring, which meant I swiftly secured the engineers needed to deliver the client project, and the company secured a £5 million deal.'

Also, aim for gender-neutral copy in your About and Experience Sections because candidates will read them. Thankfully, you can use a free online tool like Gender

Decoder to do that for you. It is designed for job advertisements but works for copy, too. Pasting in my About Section, it found it to be gender-neutral, with 'an equal number of words that are subtly coded as masculine and feminine (according to the research).'[10] The tool also highlighted that my use of leaders is a masculine-coded word, and inclusive is a feminine-coded word.

Here are a few words to consider swapping to be more inclusive, too:

In	Out	In	Out
Folks	Guys	Humankind	Mankind
Everybody	Ladies/gentlemen	People	Man/men
Synthetic/ Artificial	Manmade	Council person	Council man
Sales Rep	Salesman	Firefighter	Fireman

Of course, there are many more, but hopefully, these raise awareness and spark inspiration.

Rich Media   It is possible to add rich media to every role to flesh out your experience. Click the pencil in the Experience Section, then the pencil next to the relevant role, and a pop-up will appear. Roll down, and you will see Media where you can add images, documents, websites, or presentations. Documents supported include PDF, PowerPoint, Word, jpeg, and png. Your TA team will love it if you add a link to your company's career site there, too.

Other Sections

LinkedIn's core sections also include education, career break, and skills; adding skills will help people find your profile. Then there are recommended sections, including featured, which I mentioned earlier, licenses & certifications, projects, recommendations, and courses. Finally, they have additional sections, including volunteer experience, publications, patents, honours & awards, languages, causes, and more.

It's really up to you how much you embellish your profile, but adding the recommendations section is wise. You can then ask for some from bosses, team members and, if relevant, clients. These can give anyone perusing your profile more insight into your character and management style. If you have a Premium account, you could also add these to your Featured Section.

Other Sites

While I have focused on LinkedIn, this doesn't mean this is where your future recruits hang out. If you are unsure where else you could focus your or the company's social media activity, your talent acquisition team members should be able to direct you. For example, niche site GitHub has 100 million developer users, and Stackoverflow has another 23 million.[11, 12] Behance has 50 million creatives using it, and Dribbble has another 12 million.[13, 14] There is also Kaggle, a community of 16.7 million AI and machine learning professionals.[15]

That's before considering Facebook's 3 billion, Instagram's 2 billion, TikTok's 1.2 billion and YouTube's 2.4 billion users.[16] Of course, as any recruiter can tell you, hiring from these sites isn't as easy as running a search on LinkedIn Recruiter and mass-InMailing prospects, which often, though, delivers low engagement because people are not as active on the site as they are on others.

However, you can create paid social media brand awareness campaigns by partnering with companies like Universum and using their unique Talent Insights offering. They can help you gain targeted results or raise awareness for lesser-known companies. Their Head of Employer Branding Solutions Steve Ward shared a recent result:

We ran a one-month campaign for a relatively unknown tech consultancy firm keen to improve gender diversity and raise brand awareness. Using the right content on the right platform resulted in 6.75% of the people who saw the content leaving Facebook and Instagram to read it on the client's site, which is 6.28% higher than the industry benchmark. The result: a low-recognition firm now has hundreds of new female (and some male) tech talent visiting their site, ripe for the company to keep them engaged and in the pipeline.

Public or Private

It's surprising how many people anecdotally say Facebook has had its day. Yet, it still has over 2 billion daily active users, more than any other site! Consider giving your Facebook profile an audit because even if you don't think people should look at it, it is generally more interesting than LinkedIn. Under Privacy, then Privacy Checkup, you can set what information is visible, how people can find you, whether your profile is visible on search engines, and so on. Under Activity log, you will see 'Activity you're tagged in', including any public photos and videos, in case you want to remove the tag.

Similarly, consider whether your account on Instagram should be public or private. To clients who are parents, I have always recommended that they have one account for family and friends, which is private and protects the photos of their children, and one for business use, if they so desire, as it is easy to switch between the two. Of course, parent or not, if you don't want people to have this insight, making it a private account is easy.

Bios

For other sites the best way to grow followers is to complete your bio. Then other users understand who you are and the kind of content you will share. I am always surprised by how few people complete them, and if they follow me and their account is also private, I rarely follow them back. In the image, you will see how I also used emojis to get around the character limit.

Easy Post Ideas

If you have followed my work, you will know I do not favour AI tools that deliver others' intellectual property without citing the source – ChatGPT, for example. As an author, I spend hours adding references and believe presenting factual information from recognised sources is essential and fair to you, the reader. Other than using the Grammarly plug-in, which corrects my typos and tells me off occasionally, AI wasn't used in the creation of this book – unlike the 200 e-books in Amazon's Kindle store as of mid-February 2023 listing ChatGPT as an author or co-author and the countless others that don't![17]

However, my main concern is that people will produce post-blandness, creating more noise and lowering engagement. Just like all the poor-quality books will do on Amazon. If you choose to use a tool like ChatGPT to spark post ideas, you must change the output until it sounds like something you would say or post. If you are stuck for ideas, I would prefer you type 'what to post on LinkedIn' into your favourite search engine to be inspired by the many articles it will reveal. But I know I am going against popular opinion because I am simply not convinced, yet.

Job Posts

Netherlands-based Talent Acquisition Specialist Zsuzsa de Koning-Szabó told me that her managers and leaders, 'proactively ask me when the job is ready in the ATS so they can have the link to share. They ask their team to share it as well.'

Danish-based In-house Talent Specialist Christian Payne likes to make the process fun and engaging:

As a big fan of gamification, I challenged the manager, CTO, and my recruitment coordinator to see how many impressions we could get for a video I created for a job. We ended up with an impressive 20k views by sharing it with our networks. Before using the video, we had 50 applications; only 1 or 2 were relevant for interview. One week after posting the video, we received over 200 applications; over 30 were suitable, which I trimmed to 15 for screening. Ultimately, eight went through to the manager for consideration for an interview. The company invested in 4 more videos for other roles and departments, which have had equal success and raised Lunar's employer brand awareness across Copenhagen.

Nikolaj Gandrup Borchorst · 2nd   + Follow
Head of Product @ Lunar
4mo · ◐

New year, new challenges? Here's one for you 🙄

There aren't many opportunities to work with product in native tech companies within as disruption-ready, yet meaningful a space as digital banking. So when one comes up, I recommend that you go for it.

Right now, we're looking for Senior Product Managers to help build the best banking product in the Nordics 🌐 We have a few open positions, so we'll match candidate and domain/cross-functional squad.

Apply or reach out if you have any questions and please do share.

(Disclaimer: I cannot rule out that you will get me as a boss)

Christian also directed me to his colleague Nikolaj Gandrup Borchorst's recent LinkedIn job post for a senior product manager; it is a masterclass in writing something engaging![18]

Of course, it included a link directly to the job and an image and request encouraging sharing and applications. The post received 54 reactions and eight reposts, too.

British Talent Acquisition PM Glenn Martin warns, though, 'This works well if the manager or leader invests time adding value and growing their network because then job posts can amplify career opportunities to second- and third-level connections. However, some are guilty of not building a network, and by having minimal reach, they risk hiring from a less diverse pool.' Australian Talent Sourcing Manager Jo Dellicott countered, 'If the role is niche, I would still take a small network over no network. Some roles have a small pool, especially here, and the manager is probably linked to prospects. Also, if the manager is well-regarded in a highly technical niche market, it is another attractive factor for prospects.' Combining their advice: for success, grow your network, share the role, and ensure you add applications from other sources to the mix.

I don't want you to create a feed full of jobs, though, so I have some content suggestions below. However, as the manager or leader hiring for the role, your recruiters will love it if you share it with your network. If the job is posted on your career website, ensure the URL you share is for the specific job because you want to make it as easy as possible for an interested person to apply. The same applies if you are directing someone to a job board. Try to reduce any unnecessary steps.

When you paste the link into a new post, the featured image connected to the URL usually appears, and more often than not, for job links, it is uninspiring. Instead, click the x to close the link preview and upload a photo of the team, adding, 'Want to join the team?' You could even have fun with it; what about using a picture of your team seated with one empty chair? 'Could you fill our empty chair?' OK, maybe I should leave these ideas to marketers! But you get the idea; try something that makes the post stand out in the noise.

Side Note: Alt Text   For image accessibility, wherever you use images, please ensure you add the Alt Text. The best alternative text will describe it precisely and succinctly, isn't overly descriptive, gives information, and is how you would describe it over the phone.[19] For example, if I shared a photo of Banjo, poor alt text would just say 'dog'. Good alt text would be something like, 'My liver and white English Springer spaniel, curled up in a ball asleep on my bed.'

Thankfully, free online tools can save you time creating them. I just tried AHRefs Free Image Alt Text Generator and was impressed by its speed and result – a great use of AI!

Cross-Posting Multi-Purpose Content

If you are worried that creating and sharing posts will take too long, there are ways to save time. One way is to re-post other people's content and post across social channels, and here I have shared some ideas and tools that can make the process less painful.

Company Hashtags and Employee Advocacy   One of the simplest ways to find other employees; public and work-related content is to use or implement a company hashtag. For example, my publisher, Wiley, encourages employees to use #LifeAtWiley when they share posts on their social media channels about their experiences as employees. This kind of employee advocacy is priceless for attracting people to the company because the posts are usually organic and spontaneous.

Employee advocacy is a trusted way to reveal to outsiders what it's like to work at your company, but it can also be a litmus test for the health of employee engagement within the subcultures that form under each manager or leader. Talent marketing and branding leader Ben Phillips warns:

> *If you encourage your employees to share content that gives their perspective on being part of their team, and there is a rush of enthusiasm, you have likely got sub-cultures where employees feel suitably led, engaged, rewarded, valued and recognised, and proud to be part of their team. But, if the response is lukewarm or non-existent, it could indicate areas within your broader culture, engagement, or retention strategies that need prioritised attention.*

Searching LinkedIn with #LifeAtWiley uncovers more than just the company's LinkedIn page posts. It also reveals genuine employee posts about training, celebrations, town halls, offsites, video job posts, etc. To potential recruits, it shows the investment made in employees, the dress code, and the different office environments. With the repost button, these are easy to share to your LinkedIn profile; though you can repost without adding a comment, I recommend enriching it with your thoughts to make it stand out to your network.

Videos   In one recent LinkedIn post, Wiley's recruiter Megan Holmes shares interview advice via a video that started its journey on TikTok, perfectly demonstrating the benefit of cross-posting.[20] She could also add this video as a Reel on Instagram and trim it to under 60 seconds to add it to YouTube as a Short, all from her device.

One of the benefits of recording a video directly on TikTok and Instagram is that you can easily add and correct captions and download the video to use elsewhere without worrying about using a separate service. However, if you are using video from another source or want to add captions that are on brand or brighter, consider using Veed or, I am a big fan of, Happy Scribe because it doesn't have a problem with my Australian accent. For long videos with multiple voices, I prefer to have them transcribed by a human at Rev. LinkedIn, and YouTube will generate captions, so this isn't compulsory; they are simply not as good.

You may think, 'I don't have time for this!' I get it. I don't use TikTok and certainly don't publish on the channels I do use following any logic or plan; sorry, marketers!

However, Lighthouse Research Advisory found that candidates prefer to see videos from hiring managers 2.5 times more than company overviews and ten times more than videos from HR or a recruiter. 55% of job seekers also said they find an employee-generated video more credible than a company one.[21] So, to help your talent acquisition team, promote your personal brand, and increase candidate engagement, here are some easy ideas:

- Jump on a video chat with your recruiter and answer questions about the role.
- Share why you stay working at your company and what you're like as a boss.
- Talk about your experience and challenges and how the company differs from others.
- Grab some of your team and talk about recent achievements and how you did it.
- Share a story of someone growing and rising within the company.
- Grab a Gimbal and take a future recruit on a walk-through of the office.
- Describe how the team operates in a remote or hybrid work experience.

Don't aim for perfection because people are less likely to trust sterile or overly polished videos. Instead, include the bloopers, awkwardness, or laughter we all exhibit when confronted with a camera; it makes us human and believable.

These videos can then be sliced and diced into different versions. Hopefully, you have a marketing department to help you with this, but if you need help, try using someone from somewhere like Fiverr or Upwork. You could also bring in a video production company, like Jobviddy or Skillscout, to create the videos for you or use a tool like VideoMyJob or Spark Hire.

> **Note**   If you use Zoom, ensure the box for 'optimise for 3rd party video editor' is checked, or you won't be able to edit the footage easily in other software, which I learned the hard way!

Podcasts   Does your company podcast? It is predicted that there will be 504.9 million podcast listeners by the end of 2024, and video podcasts are rising in popularity, offering a new dimension to audio storytelling. The industry also expects AI to play a massive part in translating podcasts to give them further reach in other languages and countries.[22] Podcasts let you share expertise and knowledge, are easy to create, and can be cut into different content to post across social media channels.

From one recording, I generate a blog, YouTube video, several Shorts and Reels, content for LinkedIn, and, of course, a podcast. I use Zencastr, which records locally, ensuring high-quality audio and video; Riverside does similar. Within Zencastr, I can quickly make vertical, square or landscape videos that I download, crop, and post across sites, maximising ROI. Though I could also produce the audio file within Zencastr, I prefer using my Bosnian-based audio editor, and to save more time, I hired a Kenyan-based SEO writer to create the show notes, which I also use on my blog and YouTube; I found them both on Fiverr.

Talks and Presentations   Do you speak at events? If so, this is another opportunity to promote your brand and create engaging content that possible candidates and, potentially, future employers will appreciate.

Five easy ways to make the most of talks and presentations:

- Ask the organiser or marketer for an image to use to promote your talk at the event.
- Use the event hashtag when posting, and also use it to find and repost others' content.
- Ensure you receive photographs or videos taken at the event, which can become posts, be added to YouTube, etc., and can be added to the rich media on your LinkedIn profile.
- Upload your presentation as a document post on Linkedin or, even, SlideShare.
- Add a QR code on your final page linking to your current job or careers site; this is an easy and effective way to recruit from a captive audience of your peers!

Reply to Comments

To maintain or increase your personal brand, you must respond to people who take the time to comment. You don't need to stay online all day, but make sure you pop in for a few minutes a couple of times daily to check your notifications for comments or questions. Besides the algorithm liking engagement, which raises your visibility, it is basic manners to acknowledge people's comments. As tempting as it could be to save time with replies like 'thanks for the comment', people may find them dismissive; try to make your replies sincere.

Unfortunately, you may get comments that make you wonder if people think before posting. For example, I see a lot of lazy and cringeworthy 'DM me the job' comments that show little understanding of how challenging that is if you are not connected. But worse than that are the trolls, the people who post intentionally to get a rise out of you. I handle them by either ignoring them, because their comment says more about them than it does about me, or deleting the particularly offensive ones. Some believe deleting is wrong, but I figure it's my post; I don't want it to annoy my followers, either. If they are not adding value to the conversation and are only trolling, I will delete the comment and even block the worst offenders.

Blogging

Blogging does take longer but can lead to brilliant results. Again, hopefully, you have a marketing team who can assist you, but if not, look around for flexible help through a virtual assistant or someone from Fiverr, Upwork, PeoplePerHour, etc.

Inside Your Company

In Chapter 5, I mentioned ThoughtWorks Insights blog and how they use it to highlight their stance on inclusivity and transphobia. Under the article tag 'Life At Thoughtworks', readers can find blog posts and interviews from employees across the globe. By being unafraid to tackle big topics, they show clients, employees, and future recruits what it is really like behind closed doors. For their employees, it allows them to raise their profile for internal possibilities and external recognition.

If you are a leader shuddering at the thought of your employees being so open and active online, as Vanessa Raath said earlier, you are missing the opportunity to attract employees and clients. Simon Halkyard, a British Talent Acquisition Leader, confided:

> *You cannot hide your talent anymore and hope nobody finds or approaches them. People don't stay in one company; they have several, if not many, over a career. Companies need to get comfortable with this; create an environment people don't want to leave or will want to return to, and focus on getting the most out of them while they stay.*

Mike Massaro, CEO of Flywire, leads one of the most transparent companies I have seen during my recruitment career. You won't need to look far to see him speaking openly about his role and the business, establishing values, lessons he's learned, and plenty more.

In 2021 and 2022, Flymates could bid to become 'CEO for the day to raise money for their charitable foundation'. On their blog, Inside Flywire, the employees openly share their experience of being Mike for a day.[23] They say it gave them enormous insight into his role, the direction of the company, exposure to parts and conversations they don't usually see, his interview style, and, of course, his leadership style. By sharing their thoughts and the photos on the blog, the experience demonstrates how genuinely engaged employees are and that the leaders are accessible and approachable. The blog is priceless employee advocacy aiding talent attraction!

Medium

Medium calls itself a home for human stories, and since launching in 2012, it has grown to an active monthly base of 100 million users.[24] I post my fortnightly articles on my website, KatrinaCollier.com, and then onto Medium for extra visibility, setting a canonical link so the search engines understand I'm cross-posting. People then clap, comment, and even highlight text in my articles.

The people at German online retailer Zalando are experts at using their blogs to attract talent to their company. They link to their PMO and Engineering blogs on their careers site but have put their Product Design blog on Medium, which makes sense when it is a favourite hangout for those working in the product arena. They share a combination of posts to educate and entice, with many employee stories and experiences. They separate articles into the topics of people, process, purpose, and interview tips, and they have added a link directly to Zalando's product jobs. For inspiration alone, it is worth looking at how they write, which attracts a lot of engagement. Check out their other posts via #InsideZalando on most social platforms, too.

Chapter Summary

- 93.5% of internet users use social media, and job seekers expect to find an online presence for their future manager or leader. Many hesitate and need extra persuasion to continue the application when they don't see one.

- At a minimum, complete your LinkedIn profile and start building your network. Your talent acquisition partner can send your LinkedIn profile to candidates before their interview, putting them at ease and showing them you are proud to work at your company.

- Sharing posts doesn't need to be hard work or time-consuming; it can start with simply reposting your colleague's posts and jobs.

- Podcasts, presentations, videos, blogs, and interviews can all be repurposed into content for sharing across social channels. Rope in your marketing team to help or hire a freelancer or specialist company to help.
- Sharing your content and expertise builds your brand, too! You'll never know what doors it will open or what employees and clients it will attract until you try.

Conclusion

Whew, you made it! As an author who ironically reads slowly and has at least three half-read books on the go, I am grateful that you have invested your irreplaceable time reading this far. I hope you now have a new lens on hiring and understand why I believe, no, know, that the actual obstacles to successful hiring are communication and collaboration.

TL;DR

As you may have skimmed these pages, here is a quick recap of all I shared.

Recruitment Alignment Meeting

This meeting makes or breaks any recruitment process. In Chapter 1, you read about the aspects of the recruitment alignment meeting, which is your initial session with talent acquisition to discuss the role. Yet they tell me regularly that many managers and leaders avoid giving it proper time and consideration – self-sabotaging and creating a process destined to fail. With adequate time and regard, you will save yourself from hours of interviewing unsuitable people, getting frustrated, and damaging your and the company's brand. I asked you to consider if you should be hiring at all, explained the detriment of refusing to be challenged by your recruiter, the time considerations needed to get your new hire started, and what you will commit to in the recruitment alignment meeting.

Talent Acquisition

In Chapters 2 and 3, I demystified the Talent Acquisition function and its importance because, thanks to the internet, companies no longer have power over employees and candidates. I made the case that respectfully partnering with them and being open to being queried is the only way to succeed when hiring in a search-engine-led world where people don't have to work for you or your company. With real-world examples, I challenged misconceptions, the elephants in the room and the function's value to a company. You read about the false economy of not investing in the people who hire the people who determine the fate of your company; I gave examples of how easily they pay for themselves, too. Finally, I shared some information about the typical talent acquisition roles and the qualities I would want to see when hiring for each.

Articulating the Need

Besides job seekers not trusting AI and successful hiring being far more complex than non-recruiters are willing to accept, companies will never be able to automate it because managers and leaders struggle to articulate who they need to hire. In Chapter 4, I shared questions from some of the most talented recruiters I know to help you think about 'the need' anew; instead of looking backwards, the questions help you look forward and show you how to sell the role genuinely. To add more depth, I included success profiles from Elizabeth Lembke and questions that interviewees could ask you. You read about the importance of looping in talent acquisition and allowing them to question your 'must haves' with their knowledge and expertise; you are seeking a human, not a unicorn. Finally, I presented the market realities around compensation, flexibility, gap-ism, and boomerang hires in the 2020s.

The Cost of -Isms and Phobias on Hiring

In Chapter 5, you read about the cost that excluding or making people feel uncomfortable has on future hiring. You saw how those experiencing -isms and phobias are happy to share about it online, damaging both the employer brand and your reputation and hampering future recruitment. Through the examples, you learned that everyone in your company's hiring process needs to demonstrate behaviours that align with any stated policies on DEIB and that this includes any agencies acting on your behalf. I also shared a lot of resources and recommended reading from experts who can help you fix any DEIB issues at your company.

Interview Catalysts

In Chapter 6, I shared the commonly used interview types and explained the good, the bad, and the ugly. You read about the inherently biased humans creating and feeding the AI in HR technology and why, therefore, relying on it alone to screen, shortlist, or knock out applicants is unwise; I warned that psychometric tests should also not be used to exclude applicants. I explained why structured interviews give the fairest assessment and to include your team in interviews but not so many that the interviewee is intimidated. You read about keeping interviews balanced and equitable, the impact of your behaviour before, during, and after interviews, the importance of displacing people with compassion, and why it is unwise to delay offers.

The Hiring Benefits of Getting Social

In the final chapter, I explained that job seekers look for your online profiles; talent acquisition professionals report that people hesitate and need extra persuasion to continue the application when they don't see one for managers and leaders. You read about ways to complete your LinkedIn profile and start building your network, how sharing posts doesn't need to be hard work or time-consuming, and ideas for repurposing podcasts, presentations, videos, blogs, and interviews across channels. Finally, I mentioned that sharing your content and expertise builds your brand and could open unexpected doors or attract new clients.

Bringing It All Together

With this page bookmarked, keep this book to hand so you can run this checklist each time you recruit until it is second nature. There are a lot of questions, but investing the time here will prove more time and cost-effective than hiring based on "knowing it when you see it!"

Basic Considerations

☐ Has the role been forecast with workforce planning et al.?
☐ Is the role signed off, and will it remain signed off?

- ☐ Will this position survive a 20% or even 30% downturn?
- ☐ Should you be hiring an FTE?
- ☐ Are there any layoffs on the horizon?
- ☐ Have you considered hiring from your current employees first?
- ☐ Could someone be promoted into this role?
- ☐ Could someone transfer in from a different department?
- ☐ Is recruiting externally for this role the correct move?
- ☐ How realistic and competitive is the salary?
- ☐ Flexible, office, hybrid or remote?
- ☐ Full-time, part-time or job share?

Timings

- ☐ What is the latest date someone can start?
- ☐ If this is a contract role, what time do you need to allow for procurement, etc.?
- ☐ What is the cost to you, the company, and the work if they start later than hoped?
- ☐ What pressure is on the team while this role remains open?
- ☐ Are any of the team flight risks due to this open role or not being promoted?
- ☐ Can you make the time to conduct interviews? [block time out now]
- ☐ Who can conduct interviews in your absence?
- ☐ Who steps in first if you must cancel unexpectedly?
- ☐ Who can you trust to keep the process moving should you be absent?
- ☐ Who could you delegate the ultimate hiring decision to in your absence?

☐ What is coming up which could prevent you from interviewing?

☐ Will you be available to pre- and onboard this new team member? [block time out now]

Relay your answers to your talent acquisition partner in the recruitment alignment meeting.

Recruitment Alignment Meeting

Before

☐ Have you given adequate preparation time and consideration to this meeting?

☐ Have you answered the questions in Chapter 4?

☐ Have you gathered your team's answers to the questions in Chapter 4? No? Answer these in the meeting; give it extra time and check if your hiring partner can, too.

During

☐ Are you open to investing time meeting with your recruiter now to save loads later?

☐ Have you left stressors outside the meeting and taken a deep breath or three?

☐ Are you self-sabotaging by refusing to explain points or share knowledge?

☐ Are you being open-minded and respectful of your recruiter's skills and knowledge?

☐ Can you source, engage, and convert prospects into interviewees and new hires? No? Then why is their view of hiring market realities bothering you?

☐ Are you open to creating a fair partnership to save time, money, and hassle?

☐ If your talent acquisition partner seems inexperienced, are you championing their development or being impatient because you are busy and stressed?

Role Essentials

☐ Have you shared your answers to Chapter 4's questions?
☐ What is the cost of being inflexible on must-haves?
☐ Which must-haves could they pick up in the first few months?
☐ Have you asked your recruiter to run a search with you to see reality?
☐ Have you genuinely answered the 'sell' questions?
☐ Do you trust that your talent acquisition partner knows where to source and advertise?
☐ If advertising, can you share the salary to reduce the pay gap?

Hiring Process and Partnership

☐ Have you agreed on a reasonable interview loop to make the right hiring decision?
☐ Have you booked time to create questions and a scorecard for an equitable process?
☐ Do you trust your talent acquisition partner to go ahead and book in interviews?
☐ Have you promised to pass along feedback promptly so the process keeps moving?
☐ Have you vowed to give feedback so no applicants are left down or depressed?
☐ Did you share your preferred communication channel and promise to be responsive?

- ☐ Did you suggest the best way to chase you if you are not responsive as agreed?
- ☐ Have you decided on a rejection and offer process, and who does what?
- ☐ Have you settled on who will be involved in pre- and onboarding and when?

Other

- ☐ What else must you share with talent acquisition to make this easier?
- ☐ Do you or do they need anything else to make this easier?

Job Description

- ☐ Have you pulled this information into an honest and reasonable job specification?
- ☐ Is it balanced between hiring needs and the benefits to a future employee?
- ☐ Has the wording been checked for gender bias, ageism, etc.?
- ☐ Have you offered to create a LinkedIn post or video to help attract applicants?

Interviews

Beforehand

- ☐ While choosing who to interview, did you read your hiring partner's screening notes?
- ☐ Together, have you created fair and structured interview questions and a scorecard?

☐ Did you send the questions to interviewees to create equity and less of a memory test?

☐ Have you offered reasonable adjustments and, if necessary, met them?

☐ Have you chosen panellists and ensured they are confident, knowledgeable, and ready?

☐ Are your substitutes ready, or will you call to reschedule if you cannot interview?

☐ Before the interview, did you re-read the screening notes?

☐ Did you re-read the resume, so you know who you are seeing?

☐ Do you agree not to ask about an applicant's salary to avoid worsening pay gaps?

☐ Will you avoid questions that reveal biases or make an interviewee uncomfortable?

☐ Have you allocated enough time so the candidate can ask questions?

☐ Will you be honest with the interviewees, so they choose you, warts and all?

In the Interview

☐ Have you taken several deep breaths and left your stress outside the meeting?

☐ Are you unduly tired? Should you explain this lest it be perceived negatively?

☐ Did you give the interviewee time to settle before you began the questions?

☐ If using video, are both parties' videos on or off? Not a mix.

☐ Are you using the structured interview questions and scorecard for all interviewees?

☐ Are you grilling them or creating a space where they are comfortable and confident?

☐ Has the interviewee had ample time to ask questions?

Post Interview

☐ Have you jotted down notes and completed the score-card individually and swiftly?

☐ Has the team come together to compare their notes and scorecards?

☐ Have you given valuable and constructive feedback to your talent acquisition partner?

☐ Who will go to the next round? Who will be compassionately displaced?

☐ Do you need to adjust the approach, or are you confident in your interviewees?

☐ Are you ready to offer and negotiate? Who is involved in making that happen?

☐ What do you need to do to pre- and onboard your new hire? Who is involved?

Hiring Rebooted

Congratulations! You now have all you need to save time, money, and hassle when hiring.

You discovered that you control the key elements that produce or prevent successful recruitment: collaboration and communication. Sparse databases, unanswered emails, messages ignored on phones within reach, the overwhelm of Slack notifications, the disdain many feel for Teams, Trello boards needing updates, and so on, are evidence that technology doesn't create human collaboration and communication; attitudes and behaviours do.

From today onwards, always conduct a thorough recruitment alignment meeting, invest time thoroughly articulating the hiring need, and reap the benefits of creating a solid, respectful partnership with talent acquisition; this attitude and behaviour will keep the hiring process moving swiftly and smoothly, converting the right applicant into a new employee who wants to stay and thrive.

Finally: remember that AI cannot replace recruiters because people are peculiar, fabulously so.

Notes

Chapter 1: Recruitment Alignment Meeting

1. Cox, Josie. BBC (2023) Work: In Progress. The Toll of Layoff Anxiety. Retrieved 3 Feb. 2024 from bit.ly/49V9V1P (archived at perma.cc/V5GC-WDVB).
2. Mcmayo, Andrena. LinkedIn (2024) Post: Terminated from Wayfair While on Disability. Retrieved 3 Feb. 2024 from bit.ly/48QwMdy (archived at perma.cc/LE7X-9V4U).
3. Wayfair on Glassdoor (2024) Wayfair Overview. Retrieved 3 Feb. 2024 from bit.ly/438mUu4 (archived at perma.cc/66ME-VGV9).
4. Royle, Orianna Rosa. Yahoo!Finance. (2023) Wayfair CEO Niraj Shah Warns Staff 'History Doesn't Reward Laziness with Success' After Bouncing Back to Profitability. Retrieved 3 Feb. 2024 from bit.ly/49J0OkG (archived at perma.cc/KD3L-R9MR).
5. YouTube. A Life After Layoff Channel. (2024) Wayfair's Shameful Layoff – Can You Lose Your Job on Disability Leave? Retrieved 3 Feb. 2024 from bit.ly/49GZX3L (archived at perma.cc/DQ23-VMXV).
6. Culshaw, Toby. *Talent Intelligence: Use Business and People Data to Drive Organizational Performance* (Kogan Page Limited, London, 2022).
7. Bidwell, Matthew. Sage Journals. (2011) Abstract. Paying More to Get Less: The Effects of External Hiring versus Internal Mobility. Retrieved 5 Feb. 2024 from bit.ly/3P4veVV (archived at perma.cc/EF7X-UAWE).
8. Elzinga, Didier. Culture Amp. (2023) The Biggest Lie in HR: People Quit Bosses Not Companies. Retrieved 5 Feb. 2024 from bit.ly/4c6vs8Y (archived at perma.cc/R26U-SD8Z).

9. @DangerCupcake. Twitter. (2024) Tweet reply: Had an Interviewer Eat a Bowl of Cereal, Slurping and Chewing Loudly, During a Zoom Once. Retrieved 4 Feb. 2024 from bit.ly/3TpbHlJ (archived at perma.cc/TL44-QDG2).

10. Anonymous Interview Candidate in Pymble. Glassdoor. (2023) Biotronik Australia: Customer Service Interview. Retrieved 4 Feb. 2024 from bit.ly/3V7ESLA (archived at perma.cc/S3RN-QF2N).

11. Hardwick, Adrienne. *Oxford Review* (2020) Blame Culture: Definition and Explanation. Retrieved 5 Feb. 2023 from bit.ly/4a1C8Do (archived at perma.cc/KAR7-KEA4).

12. Scott, Jo. LinkedIn (2024) Post: No Matter WHAT Your Weasely Manager Tells You, You Are NOT in a Position to CONTROL Your Candidates. Retrieved 5 Feb. 2024 from bit.ly/49CTJ51 (archived at perma.cc/W987-BP2Y).

13. Anonymous Interview Candidate. Glassdoor (2023) Review: Marketing Operations Manager Interview. Retrieved 6 Jan. 2024 from bit.ly/3P8keqK (archived at perma.cc/W2CC-5DXB).

14. U/do0ts28. Recruiting Hell. (2023) Recruiting Hell: Job Offer Rescinded. Retrieved 7 Feb. 2024 from bit.ly/4a4Odbj (archived at perma.cc/J2PQ-CPS2).

15. Tribepad. End Ghosting. (2023) The 2023 #EndGhosting Report. Retrieved 7 Feb. 2024 from bit.ly/48JLKSz (archived at perma.cc/7F6L-W98K).

Chapter 2: Decoding Talent Acquisition

1. Statista (2023) Number of Internet and Social Media Users Worldwide as of October 2023. Retrieved 7 Jan. 2024, from bit.ly/3V5Zaor (archived at perma.cc/TM57-QRN2).

2. Workable Resources for Employers (2019) What Is Human Resources (HR)? Retrieved 10 Dec. 2022, from bit.ly/3TmCuze (archived at perma.cc/6PDD-XRBU).

3. Professor Andrew Oswald, Dr Eugenio Proto and Dr Daniel Sgroi. University of Warwick. (2022) New Study Shows We Work Harder When We Are Happy. Retrieved 10 Dec. 2022, from bit.ly/4c4XvG0 (archived at perma.cc/C6AR-UZRB).

4. Wrike (2022) From Positivity to Productivity: Exposing the Truth Behind Workplace Happiness. Retrieved 10 December 2022, from bit.ly/436ZPYX (archived at perma.cc/GJ7B-ZVBR).

5. Collier, Katrina. *The Robot-Proof Recruiter: A Survival Guide for Recruitment and Sourcing Professionals* (Kogan Page. London, 2022).

6. Schellmann, Hilke. *The Algorithm: How AI Can Hijack Your Career and Steal Your Future* (C. Hurst & Co (Publishers) Limited, London, 2024).

7. Rolfe, Stan. LinkedIn. (2024) Post: Apparently, It's the SEEK Awards Event. Retrieved 14 Mar. 2024 from https://bit.ly/3PnEcOh (archived at perma.cc/YN2N-MS6U).

8. Jarvis, David. Deloitte Insights (2023) Tech Talent Is Still Hard to Find, despite layoffs in the sector. Retrieved 5 January 2024, from bit.ly/3IKvNB3 (archived at perma.cc/HF2S-MDHT).

9. Broda, Adam. LinkedIn Poll (2023) How Many Weekdays Are You Currently Expected to Work from an Office? Retrieved 5 January 2024 from bit.ly/49VpHcg (archived at perma.cc/UN9K-XTNZ).

10. *Business Insider*. LinkedIn Poll (2023) What's the Optimum Number of Days to Go into the Office per Week? Retrieved 5 Jan. 2024 from bit.ly/3P8ee18 (archived at perma.cc/SAR6-4SPS).

11. Google Search Control. (2023) Job Posting Region Availability. Retrieved 5 Jan, 2024 from bit.ly/49ZUPHJ (archived at perma.cc/L7JJ-XD2G).

12. Nutt, Tami and White, Sarah. Aspect 43. (2023) Ethical Layoffs: Employee Experience During RIF. Retrieved 4 Feb. 2024 from bit.ly/EthicalLayoffs (archived at perma.cc/49AW-CGSP).

13. Ingram, Sue. *Fire Well: How to Fire Staff So They Thank You* (Rethink Press, London, 2015).

14. @Allaboutdogs_youtube. Threads. (2024) Post: I GOT THE JOB!!!!!!! Retrieved 5 Feb. 2024 from bit.ly/3Pa3EXk (archived at perma.cc/PL2J-RJAU).

15. Baer, Lauren. LinkedIn (2024) Post: I Withdrew My Candidacy Recently from a Company I REALLY Liked. Retrieved 10 Feb. 2024 from bit.ly/3Pad1GR (archived at perma.cc/LBT5-YWUT).

16. WORQDRIVE (2014) The Cost of Turnover. Retrieved 10 December 2022, from bit.ly/3wEsVm9 (archived at perma.cc/F4CX-KBYJ).

Chapter 3: Let Talent Acquisition Thrive

1. Anonymous Interview Candidate. Glassdoor (2023) Review: Senior Executive Interview. Retrieved 10 Feb. 2024 from bit.ly/49FS3HM (archived at perma.cc/3EYV-BYD4).
2. Botts, Rachel. LinkedIn (2024) Comment: There Is an Influx of Opportunity for Fully Remote Work. Retrieved 11 Feb. 2024 from bit.ly/3ToDN0w (archived at perma.cc/HY94-MMTJ).
3. Bach, David. LinkedIn (2023) Talent Acquisition Is Becoming More Dysfunctional by the Day, and It Is Destroying Brand Equity. Retrieved 11 Feb. 2024 from bit.ly/49FCEHx (archived at perma.cc/NFA2-AWZ5).
4. Snyder, Kristy and Bottorff, Cassie. Forbes Advisor. (2023) Key HR Statistics and Trends in 2024. Retrieved 16 Feb. 2024 from bit.ly/4chjvxB (archived at perma.cc/J9K5-ZKB2).
5. Miller, Amy. LinkedIn (2024) Amy, Why Do You Talk So Much About Recruiting on LinkedIn? Retrieved 11 Feb. 2024 from bit.ly/3T1L7xP (archived at perma.cc/DJ4R-GQZ8).
6. Apollo Technical Engineered Talent Solutions. (2023) Article: The Cost of a Bad Hire. Retrieved 16 Feb. 2024 from bit.ly/3IqpPot (archived at perma.cc/R4CE-TC7B).
7. Fuller, Mikayla. Influx. (2023) The Hidden Costs of Hiring (2023 Stats). Retrieved 16 Feb. 2024 from bit.ly/3wPC23r (archived at perma.cc/9C25-LDF9).
8. BambooHR (2023) Article: First Impressions Are Everything: 44 Days to Make or Break a New Hire. Retrieved 16 Feb. 2024 from bit.ly/3V25Owd (archived at perma.cc/FE3P-PH5Q).
9. Collier, Katrina. LinkedIn (2024) Poll: Talent Acquisition Pros, Are You Responsible for Onboarding Your New Hires? Retrieved 18 Feb. 2024 from bit.ly/3wItFH0 (archived at perma.cc/C42T-VWMU).
10. Morgan, Danielle. Threads. (2024) My Worst Onboarding Experience at a New Job. Retrieved 16 Feb. 2024 from bit.ly/3Vd9gE2 (archived at perma.cc/DCE6-LNQT).
11. Snyder, Kristy and Bottorff, Cassie. Forbes Advisor. (2023) Key HR Statistics and Trends in 2024. Retrieved 16 Feb. 2024 from bit.ly/4chjvxB (archived at perma.cc/J9K5-ZKB2).

12. Website. The Talent Community (2023) Where Community Belongs. Retrieved 13 Feb. 2024 from bit.ly/438qwfC (archived at perma.cc/U3J7-EQY2).

13. Website. In-house Recruitment (2023) Join The IHR Slack Community. Retrieved 13 Feb. 2024 from bit.ly/3wGhg6D (archived at perma.cc/4Z5L-5HV8).

14. Website. Higher (2023) Unleash Your Potential. Retrieved 13 Feb. 2024 from bit.ly/3P7XBTn (archived at perma.cc/N9Y2-CZE6).

15. Zuino, Michael. LinkedIn (2023) Post: One of the Many Downfalls of These Immediate Layoffs. Retrieved 15 Feb. 2024 from bit.ly/49DTVkA (archived at perma.cc/9K88-7EXH).

16. Johnston, Barry. LinkedIn (2023) Fire Your Recruiter: When It's Time to Rethink Your Hiring Strategy. Retrieved 15 Feb. 2024 from bit.ly/3TmhI2H (archived at perma.cc/LS6X-4TK2).

17. Hughes, Callie. LinkedIn (2023) Post: If You Would've Told Me I Would Find Out at 3 am on My Honeymoon. Retrieved 15 Feb. 2024 from bit.ly/49EbyAt (archived at perma.cc/ENU5-97TE).

18. Tegze, Jan. *Full Stack Recruiter: The Ultimate Edition* (Brno, Czech Republic, Jan. Tegze. 2020).

19. AI and LinkedIn Community. LinkedIn. (2024) What Are the Most Overlooked Skills for Getting Promoted in Global Talent Acquisition? Retrieved 17 Feb. 2024 from bit.ly/4342B18 (archived at perma.cc/WU5G-8TDR).

Chapter 4: Articulating the Need

1. Research. Recruitment & Employment Confederation (2017) Perfect Match: Making the Right Hire and the Cost of Getting It Wrong. Retrieved 1 Mar. 2024 from bit.ly/3PbfeSi (archived at perma.cc/GN84-Z23H).

2. Torres, Christiana. Degreed. (2022) Skills and Competencies: What's the Difference? Retrieved 1 March 2024 from bit.ly/3P6Zxva (archived at perma.cc/GN84-Z23H).

3. Staton, Bethan and Jacobs, Emma. *Financial Times.* (2024) FT Series: Jobs of the Future. Quiet Hiring: Why Managers Are Recruiting from Their Own Ranks. Retrieved 1 Mar. 2024 from bit.ly/3TnIwj3 (archived at perma.cc/7YBP-656K).

4. Miles, Madeline. BetterUp. (2022) Top 10 Reasons Why Employees Leave (and What to Do About It). Retrieved 1 Mar. 2024 from bit.ly/3T3GvXV (archived at perma.cc/L8YK-Z6VS).

5. Resources. Career Builder. (2023) 4 in 10 Hiring Managers Admit They Lie to Candidates in the Hiring Process. Retrieved 1 Mar. 2024 from bit.ly/49FDKD9 (archived at perma.cc/4XVC-ETZ9).

6. The Open Org Team. Open Org. (2023) Making the Case for Transparency: A Practical Guide for People Leaders. Retrieved 29 Feb. 2024 from bit.ly/435CJSm (archived at perma.cc/4LEK-QA8B).

7. The Open Org Team. Open Org on Notion. (2023) Interview Question Index. Retrieved 29 Feb. 2024 from bit.ly/OO-questions (archived at perma.cc/R9KE-ML5X).

8. Newsroom. Australian Government: Workplace Gender Equality Agency (2024) Employer gender pay gaps published first time. Retrieved 2 Mar. 2024 from bit.ly/43a0SHt (archived at perma.cc/3NSF-ECL5).

9. Report. World Economic Forum (2023) The Future of Jobs Report 2023. Retrieved 3 Mar. 2024 from bit.ly/3Pby3oh (archived at perma.cc/F64B-QR32).

10. *Cambridge Dictionary.* (2024) Definition of Presenteeism. Retrieved 2 Mar. 2024 from bit.ly/3v1sm5v (archived at perma.cc/3AEH-N3V2).

11. Survey. Deloitte (2023) 2023 Gen Z and Millennial Survey. Retrieved 3 Mar. 2024 from bit.ly/49SnnmI (archived at perma.cc/6J2R-DKQB).

12. Woods, Sarah. Altruist Enterprises. (2023) Presenteeism – The Hidden Cost of Poor Mental Well-being at Work. Retrieved 3 Mar. 2024 from bit.ly/48HxUQo (archived at perma.cc/6GFG-58YC).

13. Joel Lalgee. LinkedIn. (2024) Poll. What Work Arrangement Do You Prefer? Retrieved 25 Feb. 2024 from bit.ly/3V5FlOn (archived at perma.cc/A4F3-EVSA).

14. Survey. Owl Labs (2023) State of Hybrid Work 2023. Retrieved 25 Feb. 2024 from bit.ly/3uNPxQU (archived at perma.cc/DC49-JND2).

15. Merron, Sam. LinkedIn (2024) Post. "We Need People in the Office 4 Days a Week". Retrieved 25 Feb. 2024 from bit.ly/437xqCb (archived at perma.cc/MT6V-SVF3).

16. Survey. Careering Into Motherhood. (2022) Life as a Working Mother. Retrieved 3 Mar. 2024 from bit.ly/3v9FZ2u (archived at perma.cc/3XE6-6RW5).
17. Taylor, Lisa. LinkedIn (2024) Post: I Have Debated for Weeks Over Whether to Write These Words. Retrieved 4 Mar. 2024 from bit.ly/3v2yr1F (archived at perma.cc/96HY-K2NM).
18. Lewis-Jones, Rich. LinkedIn (2024) Post: This Is Why I'll Always Advocate to #workfromhome When It's Possible. Retrieved 6 Mar. 2024 from bit.ly/3uXDDE2 (archived at perma.cc/2WPJ-ULEJ).
19. Gers, Debra. Blake Morgan. (2022) The Benefits of Job Sharing – Are Two Heads Better Than One? Retrieved 3 Mar. 2024 from bit.ly/3v9G1Ya (archived at perma.cc/6RJM-6Q48).
20. Data. OECD. (2022) Part-Time Employment Rate. Retrieved 4 Mar. 2024 from bit.ly/3V0VYdX (archived at perma.cc/YW97-KMX7).
21. Root, James. Schwedel, Andrew. Haslett, Mike. Bitler, Nicole. Bain & Company. (2023) Better with Age: The Rising Importance of Older Workers. Retrieved 4 Mar. 2024 from bit.ly/3PafoJL (archived at perma.cc/WKH6-WUMN).
22. Mayne, Mahalia. People Management. (2023) Number of People Over 50 Working Part-Time Hits Record High of 3.6 Million, ONS statistics reveal. Retrieved 4 Mar. 2024 from bit.ly/3PaBxr5 (archived at perma.cc/9P2E-R634).
23. Bullock, Stacey. LinkedIn (2024) Post. Yesterday I spoke to Somebody Who Had 4 Jobs Over 5 Years. What a Job Hopper. . . Retrieved 4 Mar. 2024 from bit.ly/4c2mYji (archived at perma.cc/TP3E-JV5W).
24. Sriganthan, Arunth. People Management. (2023) Two-Fifths of Managers Are Reluctant to Hire 'Boomerang' Employees, Research Finds. Retrieved 4 Mar. 2024 from bit.ly/49KAsP5 (archived at perma.cc/4RQD-5HQA).
25. Arnold, John D. Van Iddekinge, Chad H. Campion, Michael C. Bauer, Talya N. Campion, Michael A. *Harvard Business Review*. (2021) Should You Rehire an Employee Who Left Your Company? Retrieved 4 Mar. 2024 from bit.ly/3T8fdQl (archived at perma.cc/SZ5R-AGUX).

Chapter 5: The Cost of -Isms and Phobias on Hiring

1. Freivogel, Emma. LinkedIn Post (2023) *Insert Company Name* Is Committed to Equal Opportunities. Retrieved 21 Jan. 2023, from bit.ly/48JPKT5 (archived at perma.cc/95LQ-Y65M).

2. *Collins Cobuild Dictionary* (2024) Definition of Discrimination. Retrieved 22 Jan. 2024 from bit.ly/49I8p2M (archived at perma.cc/J6X4-Z8V3).

3. *Collins Cobuild Dictionary* (2024) Definition of Bias. Retrieved 22 Jan. 2024 from bit.ly/3wIyro2 (archived at perma.cc/6FYB-XH97).

4. College of Engineering. The Ohio State University. (2023) A Quick Guide to -isms and -Phobias. Retrieved 22 Jan. 2024 from bit.ly/3PeaL15 (archived at perma.cc/U6VE-UMWM).

5. *Cambridge Dictionary* (2024) Definition of Sexism. Retrieved 22 Jan. 2024 from bit.ly/3PbhmcK (archived at perma.cc/MR6H-7QY8).

6. Ball, Georgia. TikTok (2024) Can You Believe He Said This? Retrieved 2 March 2024 from bit.ly/3wI0mEJ (archived at perma.cc/JUQ6-5QV9).

7. Royle, Orianna Rosa. *Fortune.* (2023) Mansplaining Makes Women Question Their Workplace Competence—And Can Stunt Their Careers, Study Says. Retrieved 22 Jan. 2024 from bit.ly/48O60SJ (archived at perma.cc/B8NF-YAKM).

8. Anonymous Interview Candidate. Glassdoor (2022) Senior .Net Developer Interview. ETX Capital. Retrieved 22 January 2024 from bit.ly/4bXfy0N (archived at perma.cc/7C73-DSG6).

9. Anonymous Interview Candidate. Glassdoor (2022) Manager Innovation Advisory Interview. IPI Singapore. Retrieved 22 Jan. 2024 from bit.ly/3Ipu3Nb (archived at perma.cc/T4XN-J6T4).

10. WBI National Study. Workplace Bullying Institute (2021) 2021 WBI U.S. Workplace Bullying Survey. Retrieved 22 Jan. 2024 from bit.ly/437Yktr (archived at perma.cc/92U8-GV7C).

11. Petter, Olivia. Independent. (2022) 'Most Days I Would Get Home in Tears': Why Do Women Bully Other Women at Work? Retrieved 22 Jan. 2024 from bit.ly/3V4ZoMC (archived at perma.cc/A6U9-R39G).

12. Women Business Collective. PR Newswire (2022) 8.8% Fortune 500 CEOs Are Women – The Highest of All Indices – According to the Women CEOs in America Report 2022. Retrieved 22 Jan. 2024 from bit.ly/3ObYNoa (archived at perma.cc/9HB7-AHRH).

13. Hughes, Georgina. LinkedIn Post. (2023) I Have Three-Year-Old Twin Boys. Retrieved 22 Jan. 2024 from bit.ly/48Iltoo (archived at perma.cc/8YA7-3ZJW).

14. Lawson, Francesca. Gender Pay Gap Bot. About the Gender Pay Gap Bot. Retrieved 22 January 2024 from bit.ly/3IqBsMc (archived at perma.cc/KHQ5-LJN3).

15. McKinsey & Company (2020) Diversity Wins – How Inclusion Matters. Retrieved 22 Jan. 2024 from bit.ly/3Sc88xB (archived at perma.cc/5YXV-27B6).

16. Glassdoor Team. Glassdoor for Employers. (2020) Diversity & Inclusion Workplace Survey. Retrieved 22 Jan. 2024 from bit.ly/3Pc7M9A (archived at perma.cc/7DJ3-KMD8).

17. u/CryptographerHot6734. Reddit r/recruitinghell. (2022) Interviewer Today Refused to Disclose Salary. Retrieved 22 Jan. 2024 from bit.ly/49HgkgG (archived at perma.cc/M7KU-CL5Y).

18. Sabhahit, Vaishali. Adobe Blog. (2023) Adobe Life. Adobe's Future Workforce Study Reveals What Gen Z Is Looking for in the Workplace. Retrieved 22 Jan. 2024 from bit.ly/3V4ZJPo (archived at perma.cc/RYK2-43MZ).

19. Collier, Katrina. LinkedIn Poll (2024) Will You Apply to a Job Advertisement That Doesn't State the Salary/Salary Range? Retrieved 22 Jan. 2024 from bit.ly/3v5Jk2A (archived at perma.cc/M2LD-Q49L).

20. Gutierrez, Cédric, Obloj, Tomasz, and Zenger, Todd. SSRN (2022) Bocconi University Management Research Paper. Pay Transparency and Productivity. Retrieved 22 Jan. 2024 from bit.ly/431Nplb (archived at perma.cc/E3S8-JVJV).

21. TUC Poll. Trades Union Congress. (2023) 1 in 2 Families Struggle Financially When Dads Take Paternity Leave. Retrieved 22 Jan. 2024 from bit.ly/3wJKGRj (archived at perma.cc/E3S8-JVJV).

22. Houghton, Ben. *People Management*. (2021) Uptake of Paternity Leave Drops to 10-Year Low, Report Finds. Retrieved 22 Jan. 2024 from bit.ly/4chnmuz (archived at perma.cc/4BXU-8RWB).

23. Perraudin, Frances. *The Guardian.* (2019) Men Less Likely Than Women to Cite Impact of Parental Leave on Career. Retrieved 22 Jan. 2024 from bit.ly/49E9F7b (archived at perma.cc/ XTX2-F92C).

24. Meyer, Eric B. Pierson Ferdinand. (2024) *The Employer Handbook.* A Federal Jury Awarded $1,675,000 to a Deaf Applicant Passed Over for Two Warehouse Positions. Retrieved 20 Feb. 2024 from bit.ly/49wprRn (archived at perma.cc/2WB6-SR8Y).

25. Feelberry Global Consulting. (2023) Jobs & Internships. Fairness with Inclusivity. Retrieved 22 Jan. 2024 from bit.ly/3Tq32zJ (archived at perma.cc/ED68-FTZS).

26. Anonymous Interview Candidate. Glassdoor. (2020) Feelberry Global Consulting Art Gallery Manager Interview Review. Retrieved 22 Jan. 2024 from bit.ly/3Tqr91c (archived at perma.cc/XZ9G-ZEML).

27. Anonymous Interview Candidate. Glassdoor. (2017) Slate Consulting Research Analyst Interview Review. Retrieved 22 Jan. 2024 from bit.ly/3P8qeQi (archived at perma.cc/4FGC-X8BH).

28. *Cambridge Dictionary.* (2024) Definition of Transphobia. Retrieved 22 Jan. 2024 from bit.ly/3P8Uiet (archived at perma.cc/ JAH9-SWVF).

29. Identiversity. (2024) Glossary. Cissexism. Retrieved 22 Jan. 2024 from bit.ly/49RF9Gy (archived at perma.cc/9RPG-XRLR).

30. Statista (2024) Share of People Identifying as Transgender, Gender Fluid, Non-Binary, or Other Ways Worldwide as of 2023, by Country. Retrieved 22 Jan. 2024 from bit.ly/3T3JYFV (archived at perma.cc/ZR2A-NY89).

31. McKinsey & Company (2021) McKinsey Quarterly. Being Transgender at Work. Retrieved 22 Jan. 2024 from bit.ly/ 3T3W41K (archived at perma.cc/VRE2-7XE2).

32. Jones, Jeffrey M. Gallup. (2022) LGBT Identification in U.S. Ticks Up to 7.1%. Retrieved 22 Jan. 2024 from bit.ly/3uVXsLZ (archived at perma.cc/3LU8-R8QE).

33. u/carrionthrash. Reddit r/Trans (2023) Turned Down a Job Because I Got Misgendered in the Interview, feeling bad about it :(Retrieved 22 Jan. 2024 from bit.ly/4c4yMkV (archived at perma.cc/FL87-8CKF).

34. u/sekasevn. Reddit r/Trans (2023) Job Offer for Deadname, Need Help. Retrieved 22 Jan. 2024 from bit.ly/3IwxnGd (archived at perma.cc/2DFC-4PTK).

35. Spurdell, Claire. Thoughtworks. (2023) Eleven Steps We Took for Trans Inclusion. Retrieved 22 Jan. 2024 from bit.ly/3T8Hq9B (archived at perma.cc/4V9J-BVAT).

36. *Merriam-Webster Dictionary* (2024) Definition of Heterosexism. Retrieved 22 Jan. 2024 from bit.ly/3ImmjM2 (archived at perma.cc/4L9P-J88D).

37. Badgett, M.V. Lee and Waaldijk, Kees. *ScienceDirect*. (2019) The Relationship Between LGBT Inclusion and Economic Development: Macro-level evidence. Retrieved 22 Jan. 2024 from bit.ly/48H2QR0 (archived at perma.cc/V54A-PFN8).

38. Burkitt-Gray, Alan. Capacity. (2022) Diverse Companies Are 'More Productive and Make More Money', Says Report. Retrieved 22 Jan. 2024 from bit.ly/3V6uiEt (archived at perma.cc/4L9P-J88D).

39. Startek. (2023) Corporate Social Responsibility. Retrieved 22 Jan. 2024 from bit.ly/3V5HUQv (archived at perma.cc/D9QM-6RSK).

40. Anonymous Interview Candidate in Pasig City. Glassdoor. (2023) CSR Interview review. Retrieved 22 Jan. 2024 from bit.ly/4c0TDWt (archived at perma.cc/W5VN-2X9E).

41. *Collins Cobuild Dictionary* (2024) Definition of Racism. Retrieved 22 Jan. 2024 from bit.ly/3TpuH3y (archived at perma.cc/BXR4-W6JK).

42. Kate's Ice Cream. LinkedIn Job Advertisement (2023) Marketing Assistant. Retrieved 22 Jan. 2024 from bit.ly/49FHlRF (archived at perma.cc/86XZ-6F4J).

43. User pseudoproxy. Blind. (2019) Racist Interviewer. Retrieved 22 Jan. 2024 from bit.ly/43460LU (archived at perma.cc/9UN4-82R4).

44. Eser rVQk8M. Blind. (2023) Avoid Rippling If You're on Visa! Retrieved 22 Jan. 2024 from bit.ly/49YfE6v (archived at perma.cc/DYH3-ARJR).

45. *Cambridge Dictionary* (2024) Definition of Ageism. Retrieved 22 Jan. 2024 from bit.ly/3P8jq58 (archived at perma.cc/7DKF-SGPG).

46. Shapiro, Jeff. LinkedIn (2024) Post. Hello Ageism. Is That You? Retrieved 10 Mar. 2024 from bit.ly/3TrwTHU (archived at perma.cc/5RHY-TA3C).

47. Editorial Team. Indeed. (2023) The Five Career Stages and How to Succeed in Each. Retrieved 22 Jan. 2024 from bit.ly/3v5KjQk (archived at perma.cc/4EVD-NKRT).

48. Officer, A, Thiyagarajan, JA, Schneiders, ML, Nash, P, and Fuente-Núñez, V. MDPI (2020) Ageism, Healthy Life Expectancy and Population Ageing: How Are They Related? Retrieved 22 Jan. 2024 from bit.ly/3wImcaX (archived at perma.cc/C9GL-P9FY).

49. Nguyen, Janet. Marketplace. (2021) How Does Age Discrimination Affect the Economy? Retrieved 22 Jan. 2024 from bit.ly/3P81S9n (archived at perma.cc/XS2R-JHR3).

50. OECD and Generation. (2023) Report: The Midcareer Opportunity: Meeting the Challenges of an Ageing Workforce. Retrieved 22 Jan. 2024 from bit.ly/3Tz9m89 (archived at perma.cc/5NA6-FW6U).

51. Safira, Devi. *Employment Law Review.* (2024) 74% of Job Hunters Are Rejected Entry Level Jobs Due to Lack of Experience. Retrieved 5 Mar. 2024 from bit.ly/435SybO (archived at perma.cc/M7VM-ZD9S).

52. *Merriam-Webster Dictionary* (2024) Definition of Ableism. Retrieved 22 Jan. 2024 from bit.ly/49Z7x9Q (archived at perma.cc/8LJM-JQRV).

53. *Merriam-Webster Dictionary* (2024) Definition of Stigma. Retrieved 22 Jan. 2024 from bit.ly/3T8EzgK (archived at perma.cc/5G2T-J29R).

54. *Merriam-Webster Dictionary* (2024) Definition of Disability. Retrieved 22 Jan. 2024 from bit.ly/48GULeX (archived at perma.cc/SRB8-YF7J).

55. World Health Organisation (2023) Disability. Retrieved 22 Jan. 2024 from bit.ly/3wImqyP (archived at perma.cc/W7LE-QKHN).

56. Wagner, Lisa. Inclusive City Maker (2021) Invisible Disabilities: 80% of Disabled People Are Concerned! Retrieved 22 Jan. 2024 from bit.ly/49FvCCO (archived at perma.cc/P3F8-HVU7).

57. De Castro, Carmen. Purple Goat Agency. (2023) The Purple Pound: What It Is and Why Marketers Should Care. Retrieved 22 Jan. 2024 from bit.ly/3TstKaY (archived at perma.cc/6C45-8W8E).

58. u/mronion82. Reddit r/recruitinghell. (2021) Why Does 'Please Let Us Know About Any Disabilities So We Can Make Reasonable Adjustments'. . . Retrieved 22 Jan. 2024 from bit.ly/4380n0B (archived at perma.cc/E53N-JNLV).

59. Stacey, Chris. Unlock. (2018) Retrieved 22 Jan. 2024 from bit.ly/3T3KRyf (archived at perma.cc/Y9QS-LWED).

60. Hastings, Michael. *Financial Times* (2023) The UK's Criminal Records System Is Failing Us All. Retrieved 22 Jan. 2024 from bit.ly/3ToL8xb (archived at perma.cc/XTY5-9KBL).

61. Timpson Foundation. Timpson. (2020) The Timpson Foundation Specialises in the Recruitment of Marginalised Groups Within Society. Retrieved 22 Jan. 2024 from bit.ly/3IrIH6G (archived at perma.cc/CY2N-U479).

62. Hoyos, Elkin. Greyston Bakeries. (2021) Open Hiring: An Opportunity, Not a Promise. Retrieved 22 Jan. 2024 from bit.ly/3wCjdke (archived at perma.cc/D4GB-PZXM).

63. BBC (2023) Amazon, Hilton and Pepsi to Hire Thousands of Refugees in Europe, Retrieved 23 Jan. 2024 from bit.ly/3v2O4WP (archived at perma.cc/C9JF-LL94).

Chapter 6: Interview Catalysts

1. Shift Communications. Randstad. (2018) Your Best Employees Are Leaving, But Is It Personal or Practical? Retrieved 12 Mar. 2024 from bit.ly/48U3Np3 (archived at perma.cc/7ZNQ-B4NM).

2. Suzuno, Melissa. Greenhouse. (2023) Flexibility Is Key: Results from the 2023 Greenhouse Candidate Experience Report. Retrieved 9 Mar. 2023 from bit.ly/4c5OQTH (archived at perma.cc/GQ2Q-9QL4).

3. Yin, Leon. Alba, Davey. Nicoletti, Leonardo. Bloomberg. (2024) OpenAI's GPT Is a Recruiter's Dream Tool. Test Shows There's Racial Bias. Retrieved 9 Mar. 2024 from https://bit.ly/3IwDqdY (archived at perma.cc/HD9A-GE4C).

4. Agai, Alon. LinkedIn. (2024) Post Comment: I've Also Been Hearing (Anecdotally) from Recruiters. Retrieved 9 Mar. 2024 from https://bit.ly/4c5YPZ8 (archived at perma.cc/NL8G-SB8K).

5. Stojanovic, Ivan. LinkedIn (2024) Post: Today Relying on AI to Recruit for You Is Like Turning a Task Over to an Intern. Retrieved 9 Mar. 2024 from bit.ly/3VbeHU9 (archived at perma.cc/9PYU-VKLT).

6. Shapiro, Jeff. LinkedIn (2024) Post: During an Interview; If the JOB SEEKING HUMAN. Retrieved 10 Mar. 2024 from bit.ly/3TiBbAe (archived at perma.cc/H3AE-76NM).

7. Shapiro, Jeff. LinkedIn (2024) Post: Worst. Interview. Questions. Ever. Retrieved 10 Mar. 2024 from bit.ly/3Te2cV4 (archived at perma.cc/9BZN-VNBV).

8. Telford, Stephen. LinkedIn. (2024) Post: These Panel Interviews Are Out of Control. Retrieved 6 Mar. 2024 from bit.ly/3Towl5q (archived at perma.cc/NH9E-EZEU).

9. McCartney, Claire. CIPD. (2023) Factsheet: Selection Methods. Retrieved 8 Mar. 2024 from bit.ly/3P7EIQf (archived at perma.cc/W7QC-FQW6).

10. u/Reservedfornow. Reddit (2024) r/RecruitingHell post. Personality Test for Big International Org. Recruitment Process. Retrieved 7 Mar. 2024 from bit.ly/3IqRlSR (archived at perma.cc/Y3G5-HZGW).

11. Wong Macabasco, Lisa. *The Guardian* (2021) 'They Become Dangerous Tools": The Dark Side of Personality Tests. Retrieved 7 Mar. 2024 from bit.ly/49TKBc8 (archived at perma.cc/HHE4-8FGK).

12. Chen, Angela. *MIT Technology Review*. (2019) Policy: The AI Hiring Industry Is Under Scrutiny—But It'll Be Hard to Fix. Retrieved 7 Mar. 2024 from bit.ly/49H5V4O (archived at perma.cc/LFB3-LZRU).

13. Knight, Will. WIRED. (2021) Job Screening Service Halts Facial Analysis of Applicants. Retrieved 7 Mar. 2024 from bit.ly/3T5hSu4 (archived at perma.cc/9GBK-GG5G).

14. Schellmann, Hilke. *The Algorithm, How AI Can Hijack Your Career and Steal Your Future* (C. Hurst & Co (Publishers) Limited, London, 2024).

15. u/Charming-Plastic-679. Reddit. (2024) r/RecruitingHell. Applied for a Job, Got an Invite for a 71 Minute Long Test. Retrieved 10 Mar. 2024 from bit.ly/3T54ndI (archived at perma.cc/2YAS-KQWF).

16. u/future509. Reddit (2023) Comment on Post: Interview Cancelled 1 Hour Before Start. Retrieved 10 Mar. 2024 from bit.ly/3wOzNO4 (archived at perma.cc/7W9R-KBE5).
17. Hari, Johann. *Stolen Focus: Why You Can't Pay Attention—And How to Think Deeply Again* (Crown Publishing Group. New York, 2022).
18. Chechi, Zara. Expert Market. (2023) Are Gen Z Workers Rejecting Hustle Culture? Retrieved 5 Mar. 2024 from bit.ly/49Y1KBu (archived at perma.cc/JG6B-NTRC).
19. u/livvykitty14. Reddit. (2024) r/RecruitingHell post. Hiring Manager's Response to Me Declining a One-Way Video Recording Interview. Retrieved 11 Mar. 2024 from bit.ly/3TvqPy2 (archived at perma.cc/PNL4-S6XA).
20. u/iam014. Reddit (2024) r/RecruitingHell post: A Friend of Mine Got This Aggressive Rejection Mail. Retrieved 6 Mar. 2024 from bit.ly/3wKDvbt (archived at perma.cc/K84L-YBK5).
21. Use Case. TestDome. Elite Software Automation Scales Hiring Using Automation. Retrieved 6 Mar. 2024 from bit.ly/3T334Mw (archived at perma.cc/UG6L-8QXV).
22. Organisation. Crunchbase. Elite Software Automation. Retrieved 6 Mar. 2024 from bit.ly/435BAdC (archived at perma.cc/NXA8-PERC).
23. u/Existing-Target-6485. Reddit. (2024) r/RecruitingHell post. Saw Other People Talking About This Company, Thought I'd Share My Experience. Retrieved 6 Mar. 2024 from bit.ly/3T8185r (archived at perma.cc/3HJP-HCD5).
24. Jobs. Elite Automation Software. (2024) No BS-Jobs in Our Organization. Retrieved 6 Mar. 2024 from bit.ly/3IocWve (archived at perma.cc/7CGJ-33RF).
25. Senior Software Engineer Review. Glassdoor (2023) Work Remotely for the Lowest Pay in the Market. Retrieved 6 Mar. 2024 from bit.ly/3PbthXT (archived at perma.cc/64EY-CC2M).
26. Press Release. *Business Insider*. (2024) Not Intimidated by Social Media Outrage, Elite Software Automation Continues Hunting for the Cream of the Crop Software and Business Process Professionals. Retrieved 6 Mar. 2024 from bit.ly/3InThf1 (archived at perma.cc/JFD6-PA7D).

27. Digvijay. *India Times*. (2024) Trending. WTF. 'Do Not Attempt to Apply Again': Company's 'Extremely Rude' Rejection Email Draws Flak. Retrieved 6 Mar. 2024 from bit.ly/49Y0fTJ (archived at perma.cc/D85K-BH5Q).

28. NSW Government Australia (2020) Simple Behavioural Insights Interventions Significantly Reduce the Gender Gap in Recruitment. Retrieved 11 Mar. 2024 from bit.ly/3VcMix6 (archived at perma.cc/2ZYB-PT8T).

29. u/Asleep-Inspections747. Reddit. (2023) Recruiter's Manager Texts Me After Withdrawing Application. Retrieved from bit.ly/3Twt9F0 (archived at perma.cc/5VQ2-K5RN).

30. Martin, Thibault. LinkedIn. (2024) Post: Our Generation Is Obsessed with Metrics. Retrieved 12 Mar. 2024 from https://bit.ly/43dJFwN (archived at perma.cc/HR7D-TMBJ).

Chapter 7: The Hiring Benefits of Getting Social

1. Chaffey, Dave. Smart Insights. (2024) Global Social Media Statistics Research Summary 2024. Retrieved 24 Jan. 2024 from bit.ly/49Hej44 (archived at perma.cc/R27W-CSM5).

2. Tegze, Jan. LinkedIn. (2024) Poll: Jobseekers, Do You Look at a Manager's Linkedin Profile Before an Interview? Retrieved 25 Feb. 2024 from bit.ly/4bZVn25 (archived at perma.cc/7TJM-W2TE).

3. Tegze, Jan. *Job Search Guide: Be Your Own Career Coach* (Brno, Czech Republic: Net Image s.r.o., 2022).

4. Shepherd, J. The Social Shepherd. (2022) 41 Essential LinkedIn Statistics You Need to Know in 2024, Retrieved 25 Jan. 2024 from bit.ly/3TpzMJm (archived at perma.cc/B7GY-GZA2).

5. Devitt, James. NYU, (2018) How We Judge Personality from Faces Depends on Our Pre-Existing Beliefs About How Personality Works. Retrieved 24 Jan. from https://bit.ly/3P8KBwM (archived at perma.cc/3F4T-CUZY).

6. Ferrari, Alice. LinkedIn. (2024) Alice Ferrari's LinkedIn Profile. Retrieved 26 Jan. 2024 from bit.ly/3V77VyL (archived at perma.cc/Q793-Q5VU).

7. Linos, Pavlos. LinkedIn (2024) Pavlos Linos's LinkedIn Profile. Retrieved 27 Jan. 2024 from bit.ly/49Yirwv (archived at perma.cc/ KJM3-RQ76).

8. Brown, Anna. Pew Research. (2022) About 5% of Young Adults in the U.S. Say Their Gender Is Different from Their Sex Assigned At Birth. Retrieved 25 Jan. 2024 from bit.ly/3V5CZyI (archived at perma.cc/4Y55-V4LH).

9. Frost, Aja. Hubspot (2023) 17 Best LinkedIn Summary & Bio Examples [+ How to Write Your Own]. Retrieved 26 Jan. 2024 from bit.ly/HubSpot-LI-examples (archived at perma .cc/7G4N-YAHX).

10. Matfield, Kat. Gender Decoder; Find Subtle Bias in Job Ads. Retrieved 27 Jan. from bit.ly/4a2OKum (archived at perma.cc/ BYN6-SAMM).

11. Dohmke, Thomas. GitHub. (2023) GitHub Blog. 100 Million Developers and Counting. Retrieved 28 Jan. 2024 from bit.ly/ 4377Pcr (archived at perma.cc/6QQP-UC5P).

12. David, Ch. SignHouse. (2023) Stack Overflow Growth and Usage Statistics 2024. Retrieved 28 Jan. 2024 from bit.ly/3T4ij7Q (archived at perma.cc/7ERF-A4G).

13. About. Behance. (2023) Be: the World's Largest Creative Network Share Your Work. Grow Your Career. Get Paid. Retrieved 28 Jan. 2024 from bit.ly/3SXrS8w (archived at perma.cc/2G6B-4TEC).

14. Lunden, Ingrid. TechCrunch (2020) Dribble, a Bootstrapped 'Linkedin' for Designers, Acquires Creative Market, Grows to 12M Users. Retrieved 28 Jan. 2024 from bit.ly/48KrzUv (archived at perma.cc/H9HX-NXC4).

15. McBride Ellis, Carl. Kaggle. (2024) Kaggle in Numbers. Retrieved 28 Jan. 2024 from bit.ly/49XLOyW (archived at perma .cc/7VBW-2WL6).

16. Khoros (2024) The 2024 Social Media Demographics Guide. Retrieved 28 Jan. from bit.ly/3P9s3g2 (archived at perma.cc/ TTE6-WT4F).

17. Bensigner, Chris. Reuters (2023) Focus: ChatGPT Launches Boom in AI-Written E-Books on Amazon. Retrieved 28 Jan. 2023 from bit.ly/3SXskDK (archived at perma.cc/F2CE-6DXW).

18. Gandrup Borchorst, Nikolaj. LinkedIn (2024) LinkedIn Post: New Year, New Challenges? Here's One for You. Retrieved 30 Jan. 2024 from bit.ly/3T8KDGb (archived at perma.cc/JU23-MUM2).

19. Scope (2019) How to Write Alt-Text Descriptions for Image Accessibility. Retrieved 28 Jan. from bit.ly/3V5DwRe (archived at perma.cc/Y9CS-FLQT).

20. Holmes, Megan. LinkedIn. (2024) Megan Holmes from Wiley/ Wiley Edge. Here for Part Two of My Three-Part Interview Tips Series For #Tiptuesday. Retrieved 29 Jan. 2024 from bit.ly/3V11bT3 (archived at perma.cc/XP59-6D6E).

21. Eubanks, Ben. Lighthouse Research Advisory. (2017) The Videos Job Candidates Actually Want to See (Not Your Branding Video). Retrieved 29 Jan. 2024 from bit.ly/48HXXa3 (archived at perma .cc/TQ5J-PHPH).

22. Backlinko Tean with Semrush. Backlinko. (2024) 13 Podcast Statistics You Need to Know. Retrieved 30 Jan. 2024 from bit. ly/4a0iSX7 (archived at perma.cc/E6VB-RU64).

23. Howell, Amiel and Coelho, Isadora. Flywire. (2022) Two Fly- wire Employees Became CEO for the Day. Find Out What They Learned. Retrieved 31 Jan. 2024 from bit.ly/438s2yI (archived at perma.cc/DZ5D-A23Z).

24. About. Medium. (2023) Everyone Has a Story to Tell. Retrieved 31 Jan. 2024 from bit.ly/3TnP417 (archived at perma.cc/ JY3S-4GUL).

Acknowledgements

Shereen Daniels, thank you for connecting me to Wiley without hesitation; that meant so much. Annie Knight, Alice Hadaway, Stacey Rivera, Laura Cooksley, and the team at Wiley, thank you for swiftly saying yes and transforming my words into an actual book.

Sophie Power, thank you for your beta-sanity edit, pearls of wisdom, and general you-ness, which make being your friend an honour. Glenn Martin, thank you for your unwavering support, years of loving friendship and contributions that enrich these pages. Power Women: Angela Cripps, Clair Bush, Debi Easterday, and Louise Triance, thank you for your tips and friendship; your banter kept me from feeling isolated as I relentlessly tapped the keys!

Hilke Schellman, I am in awe that an Emmy Award-winning investigative journalist, author, and Assistant Professor would so readily say yes to writing the Foreword for a complete stranger (#fangirl) across The Pond. Thank you!

This book would be hollow without the wisdom of the following humans, too; thank you to every one of you: Adam Cicchetti, Adam Meekhof, Alia Khattab, Amanda Lamont, Amie Ernst, Aoife Brady, Aylin Abdullah, Ben Phillips, Bianca Eder, Christian Payne, Clive Smart, Derek Murphy-Johnson, Dirk Spencer, Ed Han, Elizabeth Lembke, Floor Nobels, Gail Sampson, Gary Griffith, Heidi Wassini, Hilary Callaghan, Isaac Harvey MBE, Jennifer Stockton, Jim Conti, Jo Dellicott, Jo Menon, Jo Scott, Joanna Lubowicz,

João Magalhães, Juliette Rouquet, Katherine Mountford, Lisa Baldock MBE, Manuel Vargas, Mark Hopkins, Mark Mansour, Maud Durand, Miguel Mayorga, Mohammed Alduhan, Mohammed Karim Al Damen, Mrinal Das, Nadine Hofschneider, Pratima Prasad, Rebecca Collis, Shawna Armstrong, Simon Halkyard, Sofia Broberger, Somyen Mohanty, Stacey Bullock, Steve Levy, Steve Usher, Steve Ward, Suzanne Wolko, Sue Ingram, Tammy Bailey, Toby Culshaw, Vanessa Raath, Yanislava Hristova, and Zsuza de Koning-Szabó.

My supporters behind the scenes also make my writing possible. Richard Collier, as ever, the best ex-husband I have, and at least you didn't have to listen to this one! Steve Usher, for our treasured fortnightly conversations and your general you-ness. JB Garrone, thank you for your kindness and encouragement and for putting my spine back together after too many hours of typing. Michelle Zelli, I will always be grateful you pierced my armour and showed me how to heal my childhood trauma and gain self-love so I could live the life I am choosing to create. Isobel Gatherer, thank you for walking with me on my path, guiding my spirituality and leading me to self-mastery; I know that, first and foremost, I am an author and memoirist thanks to our work.

Last but not least, thank you for purchasing *Reboot Hiring* and choosing to read its words. May you implement the changes and positively impact the experiences of job seekers and employees worldwide.

About the Author

Katrina Collier works with companies globally to improve recruitment and candidate experience. With over 20 years of experience, she facilitates design-thinking workshops that swiftly uncover and provide solutions for the technology, people, and process issues that prevent successful talent acquisition. Based in London, UK, she is also the author of *The Robot-Proof Recruiter*, a mentor, and a sought-after keynote speaker to recruiting or management audiences worldwide.

Index